THE REALITY OF ORGANIZATIONS

A Guide for Managers and Students

The Reality of Organizations

A Guide for Managers and Students

ROSEMARY STEWART

Doubleday & Company, Inc.
Garden City, New York
1972

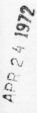

THE REALITY OF ORGANIZATIONS was first published
in 1970 by Macmillan & Company Ltd., London.

Library of Congress Catalog Card Number 76–144310
Copyright © 1970 by Rosemary Stewart
Printed in the United States of America

Acknowledgements

No book on management can be written without a debt to many people, most of them unnamed, who have taught the writer much of what he or she has learnt about management. This is especially true of a research worker who has taken up the time of so many managers on different projects. More specific debts can be acknowledged. I am grateful to members of the fourth Senior Managers Development Programme at the Oxford Centre for Management Studies for commenting on the book in manuscript. I am indebted, too, to my colleagues Tony Rands, Michael White and Nicholas Woodward for reading individual chapters. Christina Zak typed earlier drafts and Brenda Randell the final manuscript. Both contributed much by their efficiency and helpfulness.

Above all I am grateful both to my husband for his encouragement and for his critical reading and to Pat Torrie, Director of Studies, King's Fund College of Hospital Management, for reading the manuscript with such care and making so many helpful criticisms. Of course the responsibility for its remaining defects is mine.

Contents

Acknowledgements   v

List of Figures and Table   ix

Introduction   xi

PART I: *Theory*

1   Ways of Looking at Organizations   3

PART II: *Tasks of Organization*

2   What Kind of Jobs?   25

3   How to Group Activities   40

4   Co-ordination: Problems and Remedies   58

PART III: *Some Common Organizational Problems*

PROBLEMS OF RELATIONSHIPS

5   Superior–Subordinate Relationships   79

6   The Manager and the Specialist   96

7   Managerial Relations   118

PROBLEMS OF BALANCE

8   How Much Decentralization?   137

9   Order versus Flexibility   151

PROBLEMS OF CHANGE

10   What Kind of Careers?   170

11   The Changing Organization   186

CONCLUSIONS

12   What Can Go Wrong?   204

Bibliography   215

Index   217

List of Figures and Table

Figure 1   Grouping by product   46

2   Grouping by function   47

3   Multi-type groupings   47

4   Organization with narrow span of control   53

5   Organization with wide span of control   54

6   Traditional organization chart   163

7   Circular organization chart   164

Table 1   The impact of changes in the environment on changes in organizations   197

List of Figures and Tables

Figure 1. The labour process . . . .
2. Control 47
3. Workplace relations 89
4. Organisational structure, source control 93
Organisational structure, loss of control .
5. Fordist and well-being in a factory 176
6. Line management in a chart 194

Table 1. The impact of changes in the product
market on labour organisations 192

Introduction

Managers are busy people. Is the study of organization sufficiently useful to be worth the time that it will take? This question is one that any teacher of, or writer on, the subject ought to answer. It is not as obviously useful a study as finance, or marketing. Yet many managers have organizational problems as well as financial and marketing ones. Can they be helped by learning more about the subject? This book is written in the belief that they can, based on the experience of discussing organizational problems with very diverse groups of managers at the Oxford Centre for Management Studies.

Small organizations can work well with little formal structure. But as they become larger more attention needs to be given to organization. Enthusiasm, flair and drive are no longer sufficient. Creative chaos, the enthusiastic pursuit of new ideas with the maximum of flexibility and little planning and co-ordination becomes progressively more costly as different activities get out of step. There comes a time, therefore, in the growth of a company when more thought needs to be given to how work and relationships should be organized.

Managers in larger organizations may be forced to think about organization because of the complexities inherent in trying to get a large number of people to work together for common objectives. Most of them will, at times, be only too well aware of organizational deficiencies: of work that does not get done, of conflicts between departments, of failures in communication up and down the hierarchy, and of the difficulties of knowing what is happening in other parts of the group.

A manager can learn to recognize when he should be thinking about organization. He can also learn to know when he has a problem which is, at least in part, an organizational one, and can learn to diagnose what kind of problem it is. He can also get some help in deciding what to do about it, although at the present state of our knowledge he can usually get more help in diagnosis than in prescription.

There is rarely a solution to an organizational problem that does not create fresh difficulties. Usually it is a question of finding the best balance between the advantages and disadvantages of different forms of organization. Only occasionally is there a clear-cut answer that is obviously preferable. The study of organization is, therefore, primarily useful as a means of achieving a greater understanding of the types of problems that can arise, their causes, and their symptoms. It does not provide a set of answers that the manager can use to solve his problems.

The success of the form of organization must be judged by the extent to which it helps the achievement of common objectives. A good organization is one that does so as efficiently as possible. This book does not describe the process of defining objectives since this has so often been done elsewhere, but readers should remember that a review of organizational effectiveness must start with a definition of objectives for each of the main areas of the business or service.

AIMS OF THIS BOOK

One has only to look at the large number of books on organization to see that most of them were written for M.B.A. students rather than for practising managers. The present book was written to fill the gap that the author found when trying to assign suitable books for experienced managerial students to read. It is intended to be a companion volume to an earlier book, *The Reality of Management*. A book on management, or on organization, should have examples to illustrate the points made. The problem is what kind of examples? This book is addressed to managers, whether in industry, commerce, hospitals, public administration or elsewhere. Each may tend to think of their own problems as special. The fact that many of them are commonly found can be shown through illustrations from a variety of sources. Hence the examples are deliberately drawn from various types of organization, although the majority of them will be from industry.

Certain examples recur in the text. The reader may want to know why these particular examples were selected. In a book written for managers from different types of organizations some of the illustrations should be of activities with which they will be familiar. For this reason the canteen and the typing pool are used as basic examples of activities that are commonly found in medium- and large-sized organizations. These have the additional merit of being relatively simple types of activities, so that the problems that arise in organizing them can be easily described.

The computer department is used as a more complex example to illustrate two types of problems: one, that of relations between managers and specialist staff, and the other, that of the problems that arise in organizing a new activity. The computer department was chosen both because it poses so many organizational problems and because more and more managers are being confronted with them. (The author has been doing research for the last few years on the impact of computers on management and organization.)

Managers in the public service are becoming increasingly aware that they too have organizational problems. Illustrations from this area are useful to them and can be illuminating for others. Two fields of public service are, therefore, drawn on repeatedly. One is the hospital world. Here is an organization with which many of my readers, not merely those employed by the hospital services, will be familiar. It illustrates to an unusual degree the problems that arise in employing professionals in organizations; problems that other types of organization are increasingly having to tackle as they recruit a greater number of highly trained specialists. The other public service example is the U.S. Forest Service. The main reason for choosing this is because of the wealth of information about how it works that is provided in an excellent study.[1] It is particularly useful as an example because its activities are easily appreciated by an outsider.

The word 'organization' is used in different ways by different writers. Sometimes it is only used to refer to the formal structure of work. This is an essential part of organizing. Tasks must be assigned, so must responsibilities and authority; activities must be grouped together into departments and provision made for co-ordination. The extent and nature of delegation to different levels must be decided. The communications system must be devised. But organization means more than that. It must include the people who have to make the structure work, as well as the formal structure itself. Therefore, this book will discuss both the formal planning of work and the relevance of people's behaviour for organizational planning. The aim of such planning is, of course, to achieve the common objectives as efficiently as possible.

This book is designed to be read either as a whole or for individual chapters. Summaries at the end of each chapter are there to help the reader decide whether it is one that he wants to read in full. The last chapter summarizes what has gone before by describing some of the most common mistakes. The aim throughout is to help the manager to understand his organizational problems and to know what are the advantages and disadvantages of different ways of dealing with them.

•   •   •

1. Herbert Kaufman, *The Forest Ranger: A Study in Administrative Behavior* (Baltimore, Johns Hopkins, 1960).

THE REALITY OF ORGANIZATIONS

A Guide for Managers and Students

PART I

THEORY

*Many managers are unsympathetic, even antagonistic,
to theoretical writing on management. Since this book
is addressed to managers, Part I is the shortest. It
could not be omitted because a manager's understanding
of organizational problems will be increased by the
framework for thinking about organization which the
different theories provide. The chapter that makes
up Part I describes how the different theorists have looked
at organizations and what they have contributed that
can be useful to the manager.*

1 Ways of Looking at Organizations

This book is about practice rather than theory; about the problems that arise in organizing and about what can be said about them that could be useful to the practising manager. But even the most practical manager can think about a problem more easily if he has some frame of reference that will help him to decide what kind of problem it is. Like the physician looking at a patient he needs to diagnose the class of malady. It may be a defect in the circulation system, when knowledge of its working and of the imbalance to which it is subject would be useful; or it may be a digestive problem when a different area of knowledge would be appropriate. He might even decide that the malady is both a circulatory and a digestive one. Knowledge of how the human body works is much more advanced than our understanding of the working of human organizations. Even so, theories of organization can give the manager more insight into the nature of organizational problems.

Organizations are highly complex. We do not understand enough about how they work to have developed comprehensive theories. Instead we have a number of partial explanations which have been put forward by writers from different backgrounds. Each represents a different way of looking at organizations. An understanding of these different viewpoints can help the manager to identify what kind of problem he is worrying about. Each of these schools of thought has made a contribution to our understanding of the way organizations work, but each also has its limitations—often not sufficiently appreciated by their supporters. This chapter will examine briefly the uses and limitations of three ways of looking at organizations, and then illustrate how all could be helpful in tackling a particular problem.

ORGANIZATION AS A FORMAL STRUCTURE

Most managers think of an organization in terms of its formal structure. If asked to describe it they will talk about the different departments, and about the work that they do. They may talk more abstractly about responsibilities and authority. They will think of the organization as being composed of a number of levels, each of which is senior to the one below it. They may never have drawn an organization chart, and their company may not possess one, but they are likely to know what it looks like.

The earliest writers on organization, like many managers today, thought of it as a formal structure. They sought to describe the rules—called principles—which should be used in designing this structure. Such principles were, they thought, applicable to all types of formal organization. These writers—called the classical school— and their successors to the present day have discussed how to plan the formal organization of work.[1] They have been concerned with the best way of dividing up the tasks to be done, with how to group these tasks together into departments, and how to deal with the problems of coordination. They have paid particular attention to organizational relationships between line and staff. They have stressed the need for a clear definition of responsibilities and of authority. Their chief contribution is the definition and analysis of the tasks that have to be considered in building up an organization. They have provided a frame of reference that will help any manager to think clearly about the nature of the work to be done, about the best ways of dividing it up into jobs and departments and then of how to co-ordinate these divisions.

The classical writers are not by themselves sufficient for an understanding of organization. Their approach has important limitations. It is too concerned with the formal structure, not sufficiently with the individuals who make the structure work. It is a static approach, paying too little attention to the many interactions that take place between different parts of an organization. It emphasizes similarities, without giving sufficient attention to the diversity of problems met in different types of organization. The classical approach, then, has a particular viewpoint which has both virtues and limitations. The virtues remain but the limitations have been compensated for by other ways of looking at organizations, which will be described next.

PEOPLE IN ORGANIZATIONS

The classical writers think of organization as the formal structure. Another way of thinking about it, and one which all managers use, is in terms of the people who are employed there. No manager can think solely of boxes on charts or of job descriptions, he has also to think of how Tom and Bill will get on if Bill is selected for the vacant job. When the man is being recruited from outside, the selectors will often ask themselves 'Is this man likely to be acceptable to his colleagues?'

Managers, then, are usually sensitive to the fact that how well staff work together may affect how well the organization works—though they may forget that this is also true of those lower down in the hierarchy with whom they have little or no personal contact. They may not go further and try to understand why people behave as they do and what influences their behaviour. This is where the second group of writers can be useful in helping the manager to think analytically about people's behaviour.

Interest in how people behave in organizations dates from the famous Hawthorne studies into the effects of fatigue on workers' productivity. These were carried out at the Western Electric Company in Chicago in the 1920s, by Elton Mayo and others.[2] One study observed the effects of introducing rest periods of different frequency and length. The remarkable thing about this was that throughout the period of the experiment, which lasted several years, the output of the small group of girls being studied increased—apart from some minor fluctuations—whatever changes were made, including one change when rest periods were abolished. The conclusions drawn from this, and other research in the works, was that the sense of belonging to a work group and the nature of first-line supervision were important factors in morale. The Hawthorne studies, and many subsequent ones, have shown that the way people behave at work is affected by many other factors than the nature of the economic incentives that they are offered.

The second main group of writers stem from the Hawthorne studies. They are called the human relations or the behavioural school. These writers look at organizations as composed of individuals, with different needs that can be studied, and of groups of people who develop their own ways of doing things and their own codes of conduct. Unlike the classical school they are research-oriented. They try to find out what happens before seeking to explain it.

This approach to the study of organizations has also contributed much that can be of value to the manager who wants to understand why his apparently sensible and logical plans are often frustrated.[3] If he looks at a job only from the classical point of view he will think of the tasks that have to be done, but not of what it is like for the person who has to do them. An understanding of the latter is one guide to why a person in that job may behave in a particular way. The manager needs to be sensitive to the kind of strains that may be imposed on the occupants of certain jobs.

A classic study of job stress came from research into human relations in some U.S. restaurants. The study could be sub-titled 'Why waitresses weep', for it showed that in some restaurants the waitresses quite often cried. The explanation was not that these restaurants had unluckily recruited girls who were lachrymose, but that as the restaurant was organized the waitresses found themselves in a position of stress. The customers clamoured impatiently for their food, but the waitresses could not satisfy their demands until the counterhand gave them their order. He did not like the waitresses being able to tell him what to do, so he made them wait for their orders. He could then feel that he was boss, instead of being bossed by them.[4]

The illustration above is only one of many studies that

have shown how the method of organization can affect people's behaviour. This finding should be remembered by the manager who is worrying about the way some of his staff are behaving. He should ask himself: 'What are they reacting to?' 'Is the form of organization to blame?' and, if so, 'Would a different arrangement make people work better?' Quite simple changes may improve relationships. In one of the restaurants studied the waitresses wrote out order slips and put them on a prong. The counterhand could then decide how to fill them without feeling that the waitresses were ordering him about. Tension between the two was reduced. Sometimes there may be nothing the manager can do to make the job less stressful. Even then it is useful for him to understand what is the cause of the trouble, so that he will not fool himself by thinking that if he changes the individual in the job the problem will disappear. Of course, an awareness of the stressfulness of certain jobs can be useful when recruiting, as some people react less to stress than others.

The effects can also flow the other way, from people to organization. Employees can, and do, modify the formal organization. Individuals develop their own ways of doing things and groups form their own codes of conduct which are different from those officially prescribed. The manager needs to be conscious of how far what actually happens may differ from what is supposed to happen. What is often called the informal organization may make for efficiency, as passengers by air or train realize all too keenly when industrial action takes the form of working to rule. The official procedures may be unrealistically restrictive. They may never have been the best way to get things done, or conditions may have changed so that they have become inappropriate. Whatever the reason, it may often be more efficient for staff to devise their own methods of getting things done, instead of keeping to the official ways. This is an argument for reviewing the formal organization at intervals to see if it needs altering to meet changed circumstances. People are ingenious in making organizations work, but that is no argument for not trying to provide them with the most appropriate formal organization.

The informal organization may be furthering the objectives of the concern more effectively than the formal, but it can also be in conflict with them. Employees may develop their own ways of doing things to further their own ends, not the organization's. They may, as research has shown, cheat, cover up errors, restrict output, or just arrange to have an easier life. No manager should be so naïve as to believe that his plans are necessarily carried out in the way he prescribed. The research findings of the human relations school can help him to be more aware of what is actually happening.

The human relations school provides a different approach to organizational problems from that of the classical writers. It also has its limitations. Some of its supporters have claimed too much for what can be achieved by thinking about people's needs and behaviour. A bigger limitation is that although we have learnt a lot about people in organizations, there is still much that we do not understand about human behaviour. We have learnt that it is much more complex than the idea of economic man (one whose dominant motivation is the desire for wealth), but also more complex than the early human relations writers realized. The effects of morale on productivity, for example, have been shown to be more elusive than was first thought. A depressing discovery for those who thought that making the workers happy would necessarily result in high productivity.

The human relations school has also applied its research approach to the study of organizational structures. The classical school has theorized about what is the right structure. Social scientists have studied what types of organization exist in practice. These studies have shown us how much variety there is. More important, they have also suggested some of the reasons for these variations. The rate of change affecting the organizations and the type of technology have been shown to be factors that can influence the type of formal organization that is adopted.[5]

SYSTEMS APPROACH TO ORGANIZATION

It is now unusual to pick up a book on management or on organization without seeing the word 'system'. We read of the systems approach, of social systems, and of systems analysis. The word 'system' has a long lineage in the physical sciences. It can be defined, as in *Webster's Seventh New Collegiate Dictionary,* as: 'a regularly interacting or interdependent group of items forming a unified whole'.

What does the use of the word 'system' tell us about our organization that we did not know before? Sometimes the answer is nothing. It may only be used as a fashionable buzz word, which is tacked on to others indiscriminately. Yet when this fashionable froth is ignored we are left with new insights into management and organization, worthy of the manager's attention. The value of looking at an organization from the systems approach is that it changes one's viewpoint from the description and analysis of its component parts to that of their interrelationships. Such an approach emphasizes that one should not try and deal with problems in isolation, but should be aware of their interactions.

We are familiar with mechanical systems such as that of our central heating, or of our car. We know that our car is made up of a number of sub-systems, and that it is useful to know which sub-system is likely to be responsible for our breakdown. We may find it harder to think of our organization as a system, though it is probably only the word that bothers us if we think, as we should, of the organization as made up of interlocking and interacting parts.

It is useful to distinguish two main ways of looking at organizations that come under the heading of 'systems'. The first is one that has come to be adopted by many social scientists and can be called 'social systems'. It is concerned with the interactions between the different aspects of the organization: people, technology, formal structure and environment.[6] The second looks at the organization in terms of the information that is needed for decision-making and co-ordination. It traces the flow of information through decision centres. It can be called 'information systems' and has its origins in operational research and E.D.P. (electronic data-processing). It is concerned with information of a formal nature, rather than the informal information that circulates by the grapevine. The people who design information systems for managers are sometimes called information technologists.

Social systems

This view of an organization as made up of interacting variables has been used by social scientists as the basis for a variety of studies. It has been a central concern of the Tavistock Institute of Human Relations, some of whose studies will be described later.[7] They devoted much of their attention to investigating the effects of different forms of technical organization of work on the behaviour of individuals and groups. They found that the method of organizing work affected the way employees behaved, and hence their productivity.

The systems approach has taught us the importance of the concept of boundaries. To describe anything as a system involves describing its boundaries. What the boundaries are and, hence, which system should be studied depends upon the purpose of one's investigation. What, for example, are the boundaries of the organization? Silly question? We all know what they are: the physical boundaries of plant, buildings and land, the people employed and the capital used. But the organization exists within a wider system of its community, of the government and of the country, all of which may affect it. In other words, it is part of a larger system with which it interacts. Deciding what is the appropriate boundary for a particular study tells one what to include in one's study and what to exclude. Are customers, for example, whether they be patients in a hospital, or shoppers in a store, part of the organization or not? In studying the organization does one need to include them? The answer will depend upon the purpose of the investigation.

A large chain store conducted an attitude survey to find

out about its employees' morale and the sources of any dissatisfaction. It asked its staff what they thought of the wages and conditions of work. The staff thought that they compared favourably with those of other stores. 'How do you like your fellow shop assistants?'—'They are a friendly group'. 'What do you think of your supervisor?' —Again the reply was favourable. The staff liked everything about working for the store, with one most important exception. They did not like the customers. This finding showed how necessary it was to include the customers within the boundaries of the system to be studied as affecting staff morale.

The awareness of boundaries between different systems has led to studies by social scientists of what happens at the interface—that is, where the two systems meet. These have shown that jobs that are located wholly within one system subject their holders to much less stress, than those that are at the boundaries between the systems. This is true both of jobs that mean crossing departmental boundaries and of those that involve dealing with people outside the organization. The salesman, for example, is on the boundary between the organization and its outside environment. His job can be a stressful one because he has to try and reconcile the expectations of his employers with those of the customers with whom he may be in more frequent personal contact.

Information systems

The systems approach applied to information stems from the use of operational research on business problems. In World War II operational research had been found to be a useful tool. After the war its practitioners began to apply their mathematical techniques to business problems. This involved quantifying the information that is used in the models that operational research workers construct of business problems. Their approach emphasizes the importance of information, because the usefulness of the models depends upon the relevance and reliability of the information that is employed. The manager is seen as someone who takes decisions on the basis of the information available. The efficiency of management can, therefore, be improved by providing more reliable and up-to-date information and by developing techniques for analysing it. Here the computer can help by providing a powerful tool for processing information.

An organization can be looked at as a mechanism for processing information. The flow of information can be studied to see what routes it travels and whether these are the most appropriate. It can be studied, too, to see at what points on the route decisions have to be taken. A manager can be thought of as a decision centre who may be overloaded by the flow of information and requests for information, as an electrical switch may be overloaded.[8]

The attempts to develop management information systems are still in their early stages. Some enthusiasts believe that it will be possible to design a computer data bank that will integrate the information that management needs. Others argue that this is too ambitious, both because we do not know enough about the information that is needed and because much of it is too intangible to be recorded in a data bank. What is clearly possible is that some information that was previously recorded in different departments can be pooled in the computer.

The analysis of information-needs that is necessary when designing a computer system can help to make management more conscious of the decisions they should take and of the information that would help them to do so. However, most computer systems have not yet been developed to that stage, but are concerned with the computerization of existing routine information and procedures.

One of the advantages of looking at an organization as an information system is that it treats information as a management resource and highlights its importance. It also treats it as something that can be studied, like any other system. The danger is that too much importance will be attached to formal information so that the value of informal information and contacts will not be appreciated. There may also be too much emphasis on the manager as a decision-maker and not enough on his task of maintaining existing operations.

The systems approach in all its forms has also contributed to our understanding of how organizations work. It is another way of looking at them and one that can fruitfully be combined with the two other approaches. Its chief merit is that it focuses attention on the interrelationships between different aspects of an organization. The systems viewpoint also has its limitations. A study of the relationships between systems does not do away with the need to examine the component parts. An organization cannot be seen simply as an information system, as some enthusiasts appear to suggest. It is helpful to use a more rigorous approach to the study of decision alternatives as do the operational research workers, but we must not do that at the expense of ignoring the way in which people may affect the most orderly plans.

All these ways of looking at organizations—the classical, the human relations and the systems—can be of help to the manager. One or two of them may be the most useful at a particular time; often an awareness of all of them will be desirable. What each has to contribute can be illustrated by looking at the way in which their supporters might tackle a particular problem.

Let us take a common problem in large organizations, that of relations between the managers who are in charge of the local units, and the head office. This problem occurs in many different organizations, such as: manufacturing companies with a number of different works; the nationalized industries, chain stores, some government departments and construction companies. What could each of the three ways of looking at organizations tell us about the situation? For example a construction company asks a consultant who uses the classical approach, a social scientist using the human relations approach but who is also familiar with social systems thinking, and a consultant with a background in systems analysis to look at the situation and to make recommendations to improve it. Each of these consultants is told that managers at head office complain that they do not have adequate information about what is happening on the site. The site agents, who are the managers in charge of an individual site, complain that 'they', at the head office, make demands that do not take into account local problems, and that the services provided by central service departments are not available quickly enough when they need them. The site agents also complain of interference by head office specialists.

The consultant with the classical approach starts by asking a variety of questions to find out whether the duties of particular jobs, and the relationships between them, are well-defined. Has the site agent a clear definition of his responsibilities, including his responsibilities in reporting to head office? Does he know what are the objectives that he should be aiming at? Are the relations between the site agent and specialist departments at head office clearly defined? Do both know when the specialist has functional authority; that is, when he can say what must be done, as distinct from the subjects where he is purely advisory? Who do the site agents report to? Is there a clear line of authority? How many people does their boss have reporting to him? Is it too many for him to exercise adequate supervision? The classical approach, therefore, would be to look for one source of the difficulties in a failure to clarify responsibilities and authority.

The social scientist starts by trying to find out what the job of the site agent is like, what demands it makes, what strains and stresses it imposes. He asks the site agent how he sees his role; that is, the part he should play. He asks, too, what he thinks head office expects him to do and what he expects of them. His boss at head office, and the other people he has contact with, are also asked what they expect of him. The social scientist then compares these different expectations to see if they agree. If not, this could be indicative of a conflict or confusion between the job of the site agent as seen by himself and that as seen by head office.

Next this consultant looks at the nature of the contacts that exist between the site agent and managers at head office. How much personal contact is there between them?

Do people from head office come down to the site to see conditions for themselves and to discuss them on the spot? How good an understanding do people at head office have of the problems that the site agent has to deal with? What things do site agents think the head office should and should not be told?

The social scientist might also use the systems approach to analyse the site agent's job. He would think of the different systems that are relevant to the problem of the relationships between the site agents and head office. The site agent is on the boundary between head office and the site and is likely to be faced with conflicts between the expectations of the two groups. He is also on the boundary between his company and the client's organization. Again there may be conflicts between their expectations. He would describe what these conflicts are and what effect they have on the site agent's actions.

The recommendation of the social scientist might be to provide opportunities for head office people to have a better understanding of the problems met by the site agent. Like the classical approach, the human relations approach might also stress the need for both groups to be clear about what the objectives of the site agent should be and how these are related to the objectives of the company as a whole.

The consultant with the systems-analyst background would look at the nature and flow of information between head office and the site. What kind of information goes from the site to head office? Who receives it there and what happens to it? He would also look at the information-flow from head office to the site. He would be interested both in the content of the information and in the channels that it passes through. He might find out that some people who should be receiving certain information are not doing so and that others are receiving redundant information. He might also discover that unfavourable information from the site is being delayed, because the site agent hopes that things will get better; a discovery that the social scientist might also have made when interviewing the site agent. The systems analyst would try to find out what information is needed by the site agent and at head office and compare this with the information that they are currently getting. His recommendation might be to reassess what information is needed at head office, and by whom.

Top management would receive the recommendation of the three advisers; recommendations which might have little or no overlap. They might express surprise at the differences in their approaches to the task of analysing relations between head office and the site agents, but yet decide that each had something to say that should help to improve relationships between the site agent and head office.

SUMMARY

Writers on organization have looked at it from different points of view. Three groups can be distinguished. Though they started at different periods, all three are still active today. The oldest is the classical school, which has concentrated on prescribing how the formal organization should be designed, and in drawing up principles of good organization which would be generally applicable. Writers in this school have stressed the need to clarify responsibilities and authority.

The human relations school, dating from the Hawthorne studies in the 1920s, has studied people's needs and reactions and sought to explain them. It has stressed the need to be aware of these reactions when designing the formal structure. It has shown how the formal organization can affect people's behaviour, and also how people may develop their own informal organization.

The most recent way of looking at an organization is as a system. This approach has highlighted the importance of the interactions between different parts of the organization, and between it and its environment. Those who have been more narrowly concerned with information systems have shown how one can look at an organization as a mechanism for processing information for decision-makers.

Each group has made a contribution to understanding how organizations work. Each has its limitations. All can be helpful to the manager. One approach may be more useful in tackling a particular problem, though for many problems an understanding of all these different viewpoints is necessary.

An example was given of the ways in which the different viewpoints could be used in looking at a specific problem, and the contributions that each could make to its solution.

. . .

1. e.g. G. H. Fayol, *Industrial and General Management* (London, Pitman, 1948); J. D. Mooney and A. C. Reiley, *The Principles of Organization* (New York, Harper, 1939); L. Urwick, *Notes of the Theory of Organization* (New York, American Management

Association, 1952); E. F. L. Brech, *Organization: The Framework of Management*, 2nd edn (London, Longmans, 1965).

2. F. J. Roethlisberger and William J. Dickson, *Management and the Worker* (Cambridge, Mass., Harvard University Press, 1939).

3. A useful and most readable book that describes some of the findings of the human relations school is Harold J. Leavitt, *Managerial Psychology* (Chicago, University of Chicago Press, 1958).

4. W. F. Whyte, *Human Relations in the Restaurant Industry* (New York, McGraw-Hill, 1948).

5. For a good summary of some of these studies, see Paul R. Lawrence and Jay W. Lorsch, *Organization and Environment: Managing Differentiation and Integration* (Boston, Harvard University, 1967) chap. VIII.

6. The term 'social system' is also used more narrowly to refer only to the interrelationships among people in the organization.

7. pp. 33, 36.

8. One of the main writers on information systems for decision-taking is Herbert Simon: see *The New Science of Management Decision* (New York, Harper & Row, 1960) and other works.

PART II
TASKS OF ORGANIZATION

This section has three chapters. All are about the problems of deciding on the formal organization of work. The first looks at the design of individual jobs. It suggests that there are two main decisions to be made: how specialized should the different jobs be; and how far should the duties of each job be defined? Both are related to the more general question of what kind of jobs are satisfying to do. The second chapter discusses the different ways in which jobs can be grouped together to form the structure of the organization. It describes the advantages and disadvantages of different forms of grouping and suggests criteria for choosing between them. The third chapter discusses the problems of co-ordinating related activities. It describes why co-ordination is so often a problem and what can be done to reduce it.

2 What Kind of Jobs?

Many managers find it easier to think about personalities than about jobs, to think about the way in which Mary the typist does, or fails to do, her work, than to think about the kind of job that Mary is being asked to do. Managers must think about personalities, but they also need to think about jobs and about the demands that these jobs make on people. This means thinking both about the nature of the work that has to be done, and about how this work can best be allocated.

The analysis of work is now carried out by specialists in work study, in organization and methods, and by personnel managers trained in job analysis. These techniques are described in the appropriate specialist books. The aim of this chapter is to discuss the questions that managers should ask themselves before they make use of such techniques. They must first decide what kind of jobs they want to create and why.

There are two questions that ought to be considered by any manager who is deciding about the division of work, or who is thinking about the contents of jobs:

(i) 'How much specialization should there be?'
(ii) 'How well-defined should the job be?'

These will be the main questions considered in this chapter. Both must be related to the problem of how to create satisfying jobs.

Before we look at these questions it is worth reminding ourselves how large a part tradition still plays in determining who does what kind of job. This is especially true of the division of work between the sexes, though what the tradition is varies considerably from one culture to another. In some countries heavy manual work is thought unsuitable for women, in others no difference is made between the sexes, in yet others it is the women rather than the men who do it. In the political sphere a woman can be Prime Minister of India, Ceylon and Israel, but a woman as President of the United States of America is, at present, highly unlikely. In other spheres, too, there are traditions of who does what kind of work that are supported by powerful vested interests, such as some of the craft unions and professional bodies.

HOW MUCH SPECIALIZATION

The general trend in modern society is towards increasing specialization, but this does not tell us what is the right answer to our question for particular jobs. Sometimes greater specialization is inevitable. At other times managers should weigh up the relative advantages and disadvantages. They should ask themselves whether the expected benefits, which may be widely proclaimed, are worth the price. The fact that there usually is a price to be paid may be overlooked.

A distinction should be made between specialization at the technical, professional and managerial level, and specialization at the manual and clerical level. Specialization means narrowing the range of work to be done. When the work is based on knowledge, specialization can create problems, but the job can still be a challenging and interesting one. Specialization of manual and clerical jobs makes the work more routine.

Specialization of knowledge jobs

Specialization of knowledge work has been increasing rapidly since the last war. The expansion of knowledge produces new specialities and leads to the subdivision of old ones. Larger organizations provide both the need and the economic justification for greater specialization. A growing emphasis on professionalism leads to the development of new specialists who are formally trained to do a more restricted job than their amateur predecessors.

The trend to greater professionalism has had its impact on the content of many jobs. One of these is that of the hospital matron, which has changed considerably in recent years. Before the last war matron was in charge of the laundry and of catering as well as of nursing services. Now the larger hospitals have appointed catering officers —the creation of a new specialist job—and the laundry has become the responsibility of a laundry manager. The employment of personnel officers will be a further example of professionalizing part of the matron's job.

In business, and in other organizations too, there is a continuing growth of new types of specialists. In companies recently these have included corporate planners, and operational researchers. They may be able to make a sufficient contribution to the company to pay for all the costs of their appointment, though it should not be forgotten that these costs are much more than the salaries of themselves and of their, probably increasing, staff. There is a danger that the appointment of a new type of specialist may not reflect a real need in that company, but be merely a response to fashion. Joan Woodward quotes the example of the materials controller appointed by one company in the area she was studying, followed shortly after by similar appointments by three neighbouring companies.[1]

The examples cited above are of new types of specialists. This is one form of increasing specialization that takes place in organizations. More common is the increasing specialization that occurs as organizations grow. A study in the United States in the early 1950s of 211 manufacturing companies found that purchasing, shipping and receiving, accounting and engineering are usually completely differentiated by the time the company has 75 to 99 production workers. Production control, inspection, time-and-motion study and personnel become differentiated functions, if not actual departments, when the company employs 100 to 499 production workers. At first these jobs may be the responsibility of single individuals, but as the organization grows, some—such as accounting and personnel—may become major departments.[2]

Greater specialization of knowledge jobs is inevitable, but this does not mean that what is true in general is necessarily advantageous in a particular instance. One of the recent arguments for greater specialization has been attacked. It is that where there is a shortage of people trained in particular skills, such as nurses or teachers, their time should not be wasted in tasks that could be done by somebody less highly trained. Hence, it is suggested, teachers should not have to supervise school meals nor should nurses have to distribute meals or perform many of the other unskilled services for a patient. The proposal to

narrow the range of the nurses' duties illustrates the need
to consider the possible disadvantages of greater specialization as well as the advantages. One disadvantage, it has
been suggested, of the more 'efficient' use of the nurses'
time is that the other duties enable the nurse to spend
more time with the patient. This makes it easier to establish a therapeutic relationship than if the nurse is mainly
seen by the patient when she gives treatment, which may
often be unpleasant. Here, as in other decisions about
whether to introduce greater specialization, the manager
must ask himself what is meant by greater efficiency, or
by the best use of resources. He can only answer this
meaningfully by considering whether the change will further the objectives of the organization. Will patient care,
for example, be improved if the nurse is relieved of non-
nursing duties? The answer, as in so many organizational
questions, will probably have to be found by weighing
advantages and disadvantages of different courses of action; the advantage of using scarce nursing resources on
the most skilled jobs against the disadvantage described
above.

One price of specialization is sufficiently widely recognized to have become an aphorism: 'A specialist is someone who knows more and more about less and less.' As
knowledge of a particular subject expands, this must be
so. Depth of knowledge must, at least to some extent, be
sacrificed to breadth of understanding. In medicine this
poses problems in diagnosis. In business, top management
in large companies worry about how to teach their specialist junior and middle managers to think more broadly
about the problems of the business so that they will be
prepared to succeed them.

Job enlargement and job enrichment

Many manual, and some clerical, jobs, involve little or no skill. The tasks that have to be done have been so subdivided that little training is required. This is the end result of a long process of making these jobs more routine. Recently, the efficiency of maximum task specialization for manual and clerical jobs has been questioned by a number of writers and research workers, as well as by the managements of a few companies.

Writers such as Argyris and Friedmann have argued that purely repetitive jobs are not a human use of human beings who have so many abilities that are not utilized in such jobs.[3] Argyris suggests that conditions for many employees require the complete opposite from what we expect from a mature adult, and are therefore psychologically unhealthy. He urges the need to try to change organizations, so as to provide a more satisfying environment for people, and to reduce the unproductive activities which result from organizations that are unsuited to people's needs. Friedmann discusses the nature of work, and argues for the merits of job enlargement. He describes the experience of some companies who have experimented with it.

McGregor attacks the assumptions about human motivation that lie behind much work organization. He distinguishes Theory X, the traditional view, and Theory Y, two opposing theories that managements could hold about what makes people work and hence what is the best way to organize work.[4] Those who believe in Theory X—that most people are lazy, dislike work and responsibility and will avoid them if they can—will think the simpler and the more easily controlled the job the better. Managements who believe in Theory Y think that most people prefer to work, and want work that can give them some satisfaction in itself, and will work better at a job that provides some challenge.

A small number of companies have successfully experimented with job enlargement as part of a policy to try and provide jobs that are more satisfying to do. Friedmann describes how job enlargement in I.B.M. resulted in both improved productivity and higher morale.[5] Some other companies have adopted job enlargement for different reasons. One British clothing company, which had previously sought to reduce the skill content of every job as far as possible, found that this made it hard to adjust production to absenteeism. Management decided to change the work division so that small groups were responsible for particular tasks. This has helped to give the girls a greater sense of responsibility as a member of a working group and thus to discourage voluntary absenteeism. Another clothing company also decided to change its long-established policy of making jobs less skilled so as to try and cope with absenteeism. This company also adopted the policy of using small groups to be responsible for particular jobs, but trained each member of the group to do the other jobs so as to provide the maximum flexibility when workers were absent.

The phrase used by earlier writers was job enlargement. The main emphasis was on an horizontal increase in the scope of jobs by putting together the tasks of several routine jobs. This has been criticized on the ground that adding a number of dreary tasks together does not

necessarily make a satisfying job. The term 'job enrichment' is now often used instead to refer to a vertical
change in job content which increases the scope and responsibilities of more junior jobs. Philips, which has done
a lot of work in its production departments in Holland,
use the term 'work-structuring', which they define as 'The
organization of work, the work-situation and the conditions of labour in such a way that, while maintaining or
improving efficiency, job-content accords as closely as possible with the capacities and ambitions of the individual
employee.'[6]

Five studies are reported on job enrichment in I.C.I.
and other British companies. The staff whose jobs were
enriched were laboratory technicians who were profes-
sionally qualified, salesmen, design engineers, production
foremen on shift work, and engineering foremen on day
work. Each of these groups was given more responsibility
than they had had before. Each responded by improving
their performance, with considerable financial gain at the
cost only of a few days of managers' time. The lesson
drawn by the authors was that greater responsibility mo-
tivates people to work better.[7]

The main lesson for the manager, from the experience
of companies that have experimented with job enlargement or job enrichment, and from the studies of social scientists, is the need to consider how people react to different types of jobs. The aim should be to try and design
jobs that encourage people to be productive.[8] There are
no easy answers to how to do this, but we now know
something about the characteristics of jobs that are likely
to be satisfying to their holders. These guides to job de-

sign have been summarized by Drucker, for the more routine jobs, in three points:

It [the job] should be a distinct stage in the work process, so that the worker, or workers, can see a result.

The speed and rhythm of the job should depend on the man or men doing it, so that the worker can vary his pace.

The job should contain some challenge, some element of skill or judgement.[9]

It may not be technically possible to include these elements in individual jobs, but where it is not it may be possible to provide them for a small group.

HOW WELL-DEFINED SHOULD THE JOB BE?

Most, but not all, managers would say that when a person is appointed to a post he should be told what his duties are. Some argue that people—by which they mean technical and managerial staff—should create their own jobs. One manager likened the recruitment of a new manager to the act of throwing a pebble on a pile of pebbles, which makes it shift a little. More usually, the disagreement is about how specifically one should spell out job responsibilities. Those who favour doing so in considerable detail argue that it is the only way to avoid ambiguities, and to ensure that all the work that needs doing has been analysed and assigned. It is also, they point out, useful to do so as a framework for appraising performance. Those who object to a detailed description of responsibilities say that it makes people take too narrow a view of their job as being necessarily bounded by and limited to the specified responsibilities, when other work may need to be done. They may also object because they think that the rapidity of change makes job descriptions rapidly out of date and so of little value.

A good argument in support of job descriptions is that they force the compiler to think more clearly about the functions of a job. This is most necessary when an appointment is going to be made. Management may merely say: 'We need a good man in the sales department', but unless they think why they need a good man and what they want him to do they will not know what kind of man they should be looking for, nor how his job is to fit in with existing jobs. The preparation of a job description can help to ensure that they are asking themselves the right questions.

Dale suggests that, 'as a business grows larger, each person should at least be given instructions on:

(i) the objective of the whole organization (company, division or at least department) and the part he is expected to play in reaching it;

(ii) whom he has line authority over, and who has line authority over him;

(iii) his relationships with others on his own level—specifically, he should be able to get the information or co-operation he needs from others as a right and not as a favour;

(iv) the deadlines it is necessary to observe if other segments of the organizations are to meet their objectives.[10]

Dale's list is an interesting one as the last two points are often omitted from job descriptions. The third point is probably optimistic in that there are likely to be times when a manager needs information or co-operation but can only get it as a favour, however carefully worded his job description. Even so, it is a useful reminder of how much manager's work may depend upon his relationships with others who are not in the straight-line hierarchy. The fourth point on deadlines seems a desirable addition in underlining where the responsibility lies, but as any editor and many computer managers know, awareness of deadlines does not necessarily mean that people consider meeting them of much importance.

The traditional job description can be criticized for not being sufficiently informative. Dale, as we have seen, made two points that are not usually included in a list of job responsibilities. Chapple and Sayles produced a job description which gave the work flow. They argued that a job description should say what the manager does, with whom, when, where and how often, instead of using vague phrases like 'work with'.[11]

Job descriptions are only one aspect of formalization. There is the broader question of how far, if at all, the job can or should be moulded or even made by the man who occupies it. The more scope there is for initiative in a job—that is, the less the requirements of the job are precisely defined—the more the man can make the job. The United States Presidency is an outstanding example of this. The extent to which an individual can mould the job usually depends on the level of the job and on the type of organization, as well as on the individual's own abilities. In general, the more senior the job the more opportunities there are for the individual to give it his personal signature. The managing director has the greatest scope for doing so as he can decide which aspects of this varied job he thinks most important or finds most congenial. His choice will often be determined by his own functional background. An accountant is likely to see the job of a managing director in a different way from that of a former head of the research department. The scope for the individual to shape the job will also depend on how bureaucratic is the organization for which he works. A very bureaucratic organization will have precise terms of reference for each job and may not allow managers any say in the appointment of their staff—one of the ways in which a man can determine the character of his department or section.

The smaller is the organization the more the man may have to be allowed to change or even to create the job. In a very large organization there is likely, except for the top posts, to be a clearly-shaped hole to be filled. In medium-sized organizations there is more choice between a policy of fitting men to jobs and one of allowing men to make their own jobs. In all organizations there is some choice between the two. What choice is made will probably be partly determined by management philosophy and partly by the organization's need for stability or flexibility.

A manager who has to decide whether he thinks jobs should be strictly defined should ask himself: 'Do I believe that people should be allowed scope to make the job that suits their abilities?' 'Do I believe in telling people what the needs are and then leaving it to them to decide how they should best be met?' 'Do I believe that the uncertainties and frictions that such a belief is likely to create between managers are more fruitful than harmful?' The man who says 'Yes' to these questions will seek to appoint good men and expect them to, at least in part, create their own jobs. The man who favours the classical approach to organization, or who is temperamentally in favour of order and clarity, will believe that it is better to describe clearly what are the responsibilities and duties of each job, and how these are related to other jobs. He will believe in defining the job and then looking for a suitable man to fill it.

The individual who is looking for a job needs to think what kind of organization will suit his temperament best. Does he feel happier if he knows where he is? If his relations with other people are part of a prescribed pattern? Or does he want to be free to exercise as much initiative as possible, to create his own job? It is important that both those who are filling jobs and those who are looking for them should know which type of job it is and, therefore, what kind of person is suitable for it.

The question of whether the man should fit the job or the job the man is only one aspect of the wider problem of how formalized should the organization be—that is, how far positions, tasks and procedures should be formally laid down. This, one of the major problems of organization, will be discussed in a later chapter.

SUMMARY

Most managers need at times to think about the content of a particular job. They should ask themselves what kind of jobs they want to create and why?

One characteristic of jobs is how specialized they are. Increasing knowledge, the growth in the size of organizations and a greater emphasis on professionalism have all led to more specialization of managerial and technical jobs. This is often inevitable, but the manager should always ask himself whether it is desirable in a particular instance.

There has been a long process of making manual and clerical jobs more specialized by reducing their skill content. Recently the desirability of doing so has been questioned by some writers who have argued that many such jobs make unproductive use of human beings and create undesirable reactions in consequence. A few companies have experimented with various methods of increasing the scope of jobs. They have reported increases in productivity. The characteristics that a relatively routine job should have if it is likely to be a satisfying one, for the man or woman doing it, are described.

Managers have to decide how far the duties of a job should be defined. The size of the organization, and the position in the hierarchy, will affect the amount of flexibility that is possible. So will the organization's relative need for order compared with flexibility. Much can also depend on top management's philosophy. In general does it believe that a man should be free to make the job or that he should be selected to fit a well-defined post?

.   .   .

1. Joan Woodward, *Industrial Organization: Theory and Practice* (London, Oxford University Press, 1965) p. 22.

2. A. W. Baker and R. C. Davis, *Ratios of Staff to Works Employees and Stages of Differentiation of Staff Functions* (Columbia, Ohio State University, Bureau of Business Research, Monograph No. 72, 1954).

3. Chris Argyris, *Personality and Organization* (New York, Harper Bros, 1957); *Integrating the Individual and the Organization* (New York, John Wiley, 1964); Georges Friedmann, *The Anatomy of Work: The Implications of Specialization* (London, Heinemann, 1961).

4. Douglas McGregor, *The Human Side of Enterprise* (London, McGraw-Hill, 1960).

5. Friedmann, *Anatomy of Work*, pp. 43–8.

6. *Work-Structuring: A Summary of Experiments at Philips–* 1963–8 (Personnel and Industrial Relations and the Technical Efficiency and Organization Departments of N.V. Philips's Gloeilampenfabrieken, Holland; an internal booklet) p. 4.

7. William J. Paul Jr, Keith B. Robertson and Frederick Herzberg, 'Job Enrichment Pays Off', *Harvard Business Review* (Mar– Apr 1969).

8. A good book on the subject is Frederick Herzberg's *Work and the Nature of Man* (London, Staples, 1968).

9. Peter Drucker, *The Practice of Management* (London, Pan Books, 1968), pp. 235 ff.

10. Ernest Dale, *Organization* (American Management Association, 1967) p. 140.

11. Eliot D. Chapple and Leonard R. Sayles, *The Measure of Management: Designing Organizations for Human Effectiveness* (New York, The Macmillan Co., 1961), chap. 2, pp. 18 ff.

3 How to Group Activities

Jobs in organizations cannot exist in isolation. They have to be related to each other. This is called 'grouping' or, an even more unappealing word, 'departmentalization'. This chapter is about the different ways in which work can be grouped, and the criteria that managers should use to help them decide which is the most appropriate for their circumstances. Unfortunately it is a dull subject, but a necessary task of organization.

Sometimes the grouping of jobs causes no problems. In a canteen the waitresses will clearly be grouped together, so will the kitchen staff. Both groups will report to their own supervisor, who will report in turn to the canteen manager. So far there are few or no problems in deciding the right form of grouping. But who should the canteen manager report to? There may be no obvious answer. In companies it is often the personnel manager, but may be the works manager or the head of administrative services. It may not matter much what decision is made as the canteen is a relatively self-contained activity, which is unlikely to be much affected by the place of its manager in the organization. There may even be a reluctance to be responsible for the canteen as it is more likely to be a source of grievance than of praise.

The problem of finding the best place for the computer department in the organization is much more complex than the canteen. It is a new activity, so there is no traditional answer. It is also an activity that can affect a variety of other departments, so it has no obvious departmental home. Some new activities have, such as psychological testing in a company, which would clearly be put in personnel. Unlike the canteen, what the computer department does will depend, in part, on where it is in the organization. This is an argument against putting the computer under the control of the finance department, as is frequently done, because doing so may discourage other departments from making adequate use of it. The decision about grouping of an activity matters most when the nature of that activity will be affected by it.

TYPES OF GROUPING

A manager who has to decide where to place an activity in the organization will find it useful to know what types of grouping are available and what are their advantages and disadvantages. A knowledge of the types of grouping becomes still more important when the manager is thinking about building a new organization or reorganizing an existing one. The main types of groupings are described below.

Products or services[1]

Different products made by the same company may require their own specialized equipment and their own expertise. Where this is so, grouping by product is often found to be a convenient way of dividing up the company into fairly self-contained parts. It is, of course, most common in large diversified companies where there is more likely to be a wish to reduce some of the problems of size by creating semi-autonomous units. The advantages of this type of grouping is that it brings together all those with special knowledge of the product, and makes for easier co-ordination of activities like purchase, production and sales that are associated with it. Grouping by product is also often used within a department, as when the sales or purchasing departments are subdivided into sections for each of the main products.

All the activities associated with a particular service may also be grouped together, as they are in the simple example of a typing pool or as they may be in the computer or transport departments (it can be argued that this is also functional grouping, which is described below). Whether to create separate service departments or to provide each establishment or department with its own services is one of the common problems in large organizations. Managers often prefer to have control over the services they use, such as typing, engineering or personnel. Services that need expensive communal equipment such as canteens and computers, or that must work to very stringent standards, may need to be grouped together more than services that can be rendered by individuals with their own equipment like typewriters.

Functions[2]

This is the most commonly used basis for grouping in all types of organizations.[3] In some, where the heads of the main functional departments report to the chief executive, it is the dominant one. In others it is a subsidiary one, as it is in a product division, where the general manager may have functional heads reporting to him. The typical functions of a manufacturing company are: production, sales, engineering, accounting, purchasing and personnel. In some manufacturing companies research and development is essential and so must be a separate function. The relative importance of sales—now increasingly called 'marketing' after United States' practice—varies greatly from one type of business to another, so will the size of the department and its relative importance in the hierarchy. Only a careful analysis of the activities of the organization will show one which are sufficiently important to be organized as separate functions.

Specialization is the main advantage of grouping by function. It brings together the specialized knowledge needed for that particular activity. It also helps to ensure that adequate attention is given to it. The latter is the reason for the creation of new functional departments, such as public relations. Specialization, as we saw in the last chapter, also has its disadvantages. It can make people narrow-minded so that they concentrate on their own speciality and know and care little about the other activities in their organization. There is always the danger in functional grouping that people will put the interests of their own function above that of the organization as a whole. The larger the organization the greater the danger that functional grouping will lead to the growth of specialized and myopic departments that are hard to co-ordinate. Hence the creation of separate product groups in many large manufacturing companies, and the use of functional grouping as a subsidiary rather than as the main form of departmentalization.

The definition of a function is very general and does not tell one what particular activities will be included in it. So to say, for example, that one is going to group personnel activities together does not tell one what will be included in the personnel department. Will it include training? Salaries—which the accounting department may wish to retain? Therefore, to decide that one is going to set up a functional group is no substitute for clear thinking about what activities it should contain.

Customers

Grouping by customers means separate groups for different types of customers. This form of organization is most appropriate in sales departments that sell to very different markets, such as domestic and industrial consumers or home and export sales. Separate grouping enables their particular requirements to be catered for more knowledgeably. The same applies to the distinction made by the Department of Employment and Productivity between employment services provided for those under eighteen years old and those for adults. In hospitals, similarly, there are medical and surgical wards, also wards for men, women and children.

Canteens lend themselves to a variety of different types of customer grouping. The choices are: one canteen for everyone; several canteens open to all but providing different standards at different prices—grouping by service; grouping by different types of customers, either by type of work—clean and dirty—by level in the hierarchy, or, as in some hospitals, by function. There may also, in a large spread-out works, be canteens in different locations. This is grouping by place, which is discussed below.

The decision that is made about the canteen will, as in most grouping decisions, have to weigh a number of considerations. Is it desirable to provide one category of employees with a higher standard of food and service than another category, or to provide lower-paid employees with a cheaper meal than higher-paid staff? Should one make it easier for one group of employees to talk together at mealtimes although this reduces the opportunities for them to have informal contacts with other groups? Another consideration is what are the preferences of the different groups. These may vary from one type of organization to another and from one part of the country to another. Workers may prefer to eat separately from their bosses. Managers may think a high-grade manager's dining-room an essential promotion perk. When customer grouping is bedevilled by status feelings it is much harder to decide what is the best organization! Even if the decision is to have the same canteen for everyone, management may find that, in practice, employees segregate themselves by coming in at different times or by sitting at different tables.

Place

This is an important basis for grouping where services to customers or clients can most economically be provided within a limited distance, or where—as in a hospital, school or post office—it is most convenient for the customer if the service is near by. Customer convenience, though, may be overridden by other considerations such as economy.

It may be easy to decide that grouping by place is necessary for some consumer goods and services. The more difficult problem is to decide on what is the right size for an area. This problem arises in an acute form in discussions on regionalization and the right pattern for local government.

Time

Organizations that employ workers on shifts, whether

in industry, hospitals or elsewhere, will have separate groups for the different shifts. Should each shift do the same kind of work? The answer may be clearly 'Yes', as in continuous shift-working, though more maintenance may be done on one shift than another. Should different shifts do different tasks? There may be no choice; night nursing is bound to be different from day nursing. In the computer department that is on three shifts, longer and more straightforward runs will be done at night as they should generate fewer queries. In some forms of organization there may be more choice as to what each shift should do. Trist and Bamforth found that one of the troubles with the conventional long-wall method of coal-mining was that each shift was responsible for a different phase of coal-getting, and that this contributed to the friction that existed between the shifts. Relations were much better when groups of workers, with members in each shift, were made responsible for a work cycle.[4]

Organization charts can show one which type or types of grouping has been adopted. Figure 1 shows grouping by product of a diversified company, Figure 2, grouping

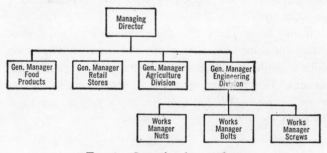

Fig. 1   Grouping by product

by function. Figure 3 illustrates how a number of different types of grouping—product, function and area—may be used in the same organization. In this illustration product grouping is the primary one.

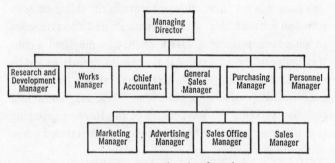

FIG. 2   Grouping by function

Most organizations contain examples of several of these types of grouping. How can a manager decide which type or combination of types is best? There are no definite

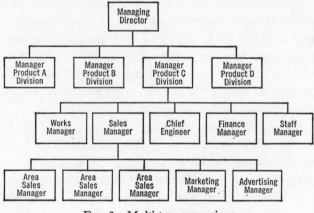

FIG. 3   Multi-type groupings

answers, but among the large number of different criteria which have been suggested, the ones described below seem the most useful.

It is helpful for the manager to examine his plans for grouping against these different criteria, as doing so may give him a better idea of the advantages and disadvantages of what he is proposing. Unfortunately he may find a conflict between the criteria. All he can do then is to try to choose the grouping which best seems to suit the present needs of his particular organization. Time may show him that he overrated the advantages of the form of grouping that he chose and that he overlooked or underrated some of the disadvantages.

CRITERIA FOR GROUPING

Good co-ordination

This is a major problem in most organizations, so the type of grouping that will minimize the problem must have a lot to be said for it. The larger the organization the more weight must be given to this criterion. This is why, as we saw above, the specialist advantages of functional grouping may be outweighed in large organizations by the disadvantages of poor co-ordination.

Two other criteria, which are sometimes given, can be put under the general heading of co-ordination. One is the criterion of use, which suggests that activities should be grouped around the main users. The other criterion is control, which suggests that activities should be grouped where they can most easily be controlled.

Economy

The relative costs of different forms of grouping is another factor that should be considered. Other criteria may outweigh the arguments for economy, but at least the costs of alternative forms of grouping should, as far as possible, be assessed. For example, one form of grouping may need more equipment than another, more staff, or use more expensive office space. Some organizations, both business and Civil Service, have moved part of their staff out of London after deciding that some activities were sufficiently self-contained that they could be physically separated from the expensive London offices.

Use of specialist knowledge

Grouping by product brings together those with specialist knowledge of the product. Grouping by type of customer puts the emphasis on specialist knowledge of a particular type of customer. The manager should decide how important specialist knowledge is, and which kind of specialist knowledge is most useful. Where specialist knowledge is in short supply this criterion will have extra weight.

Clarity of division of work

The grouping should, as far as possible, avoid ambiguity about the work to be done, and who should do it. Such ambiguity will increase the problems of co-ordination, so this criterion is related to the first. Uncertainty as to which department or which section is responsible for work can lead to conflict. This is most likely to arise at the boundaries between groupings. Hence the desirability, where possible, of dividing the groups by some clear-cut criterion. Uncertainty cannot always be avoided, but the method of grouping should try to minimize it. However, there may also, as we saw in the discussion on job descriptions, be dangers in too precise and rigid a definition of who does what. It can, for instance, cause delay if the man on the spot says: 'It is not my job to do so and so.'

Minimizing conflict

Disharmonies and inefficiencies can arise from a grouping that has been made purely from technical considerations without regard to the effects that it has on the workers involved. This has been shown in research by members of the Tavistock Institute of Human Relations. They used the phrase 'socio-technical systems' to describe the fact 'that any production system requires both a technological organization—equipment and process layout—and a work organization relating to each other those who carry out the necessary tasks'.[5] Sometimes the technical requirements may not allow alternative work groupings, but where they do the manager should try and take into account the likely effects of different types of grouping on relationships between the workers and between them and their supervisors.

The criterion of avoiding conflict should also be applied to the grouping of new activities. Those responsible for the organizational decision should ask themselves: 'What benefits does control of this activity confer?' For example the question should be asked of the planning and computer departments, both of which may in time affect the relative status of departments. As managers become more aware of the potentialities of computers they

may see control of the computer and its associated personnel as an important new tool in the power struggle
with other managers. In some companies they already do
so.

Appreciation of local conditions
The need to recognize local conditions is one of the
reasons for grouping by place. It is an important consideration in some sales and service organizations.

The relative importance of these different criteria will
depend upon one's aims. If one is clear about the purpose
of an activity it is easier to decide how much weight to
give to the different criteria. A change in purpose may
lead to a change in their relative importance. The purpose of mental hospitals, for example, has been changing
from that of predominantly custodial institutions, when
the organization of separate and geographically remote
units was thought appropriate, to therapeutic, often short-
stay hospitals which can be included in a general hospital.

DIVISIONALIZATION
This has become increasingly popular with many large
companies, which have sought to decentralize by breaking the organization up into semi-autonomous parts. Divisions, which may be subsidiary companies, may be based
on functions, geographical area or product. The American Management Association's study in the mid-1960s
showed that most large and many medium-sized companies were divisionalized.[6] Divisionalization, like other
forms of decentralization, brings decision-making nearer

to the scene of action. It also makes it easier to assign accountability for these self-contained divisions.

The A.M.A. study showed that the companies which did not divisionalize had some or all of the following characteristics:

A few large customers } A few large suppliers }	which could most conveniently be dealt with by one organizational unit
Products with closely related technologies	which made division by product undesirable
Large-scale production and slowly changing technology	which made decentralization less necessary, and hence also divisionalization.

Such companies were found in some of the process industries, chiefly steel, cement, oil and paper.

SPAN OF CONTROL (HOW MANY TO A BOSS?)

A different type of problem in grouping jobs together, from those described so far, is that of 'How many jobs should be put under one supervisor or manager?' This is the much-discussed 'span of control'.[7] As Urwick put it: 'No person should supervise more than five, or at most six direct subordinates whose work interlocks.'[8] Few people nowadays would accept this as it stands, but all would probably think that there are limits to the number of people who can be effectively supervised by one person. What these limits are in any particular situation will depend both upon its characteristics and upon management aims. If detailed control, for example, is considered desirable the manager, unless he is in a position to provide precise instructions, should only have a few subordinates. In general, the more decentralized the organization the more possible it is to increase the span of control.

There are numerous factors to be considered in the situation itself. One of the most important is the experience and knowledge of the people being supervised, hence the extent to which they may need supervision. Another is the difficulty of the work being done. The more routine the jobs the greater usually can be the number of people supervised, so at the bottom of the hierarchy, whether on the shop floor or in the office, one is likely to find larger spans of control than higher up. Urwick's principle showed another factor that is important—that is, the extent to which the subordinate's work interlocks. The area manager in charge of managers of stores in different towns will only be dealing with their work individually, whereas the manager of a group of people who are in frequent contact with each other will also have to deal with their relations with each other. Any manager will know what problems this can bring!

The span of control that is chosen will affect the number of levels in the organization. The narrower the span of control the more levels there will be. The organization chart will then look like a steep pyramid as in Figure 4.

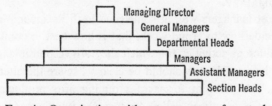

FIG. 4 Organization with narrow span of control

An organization with wide spans of control will have a much flatter pyramid, with fewer levels, as in Figure 5. It will also provide jobs with more scope than in an organization with a narrow span of control and many tiers. Com-

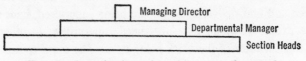

FIG. 5   Organization with wide span of control

munications upwards and downwards are likely to be more difficult where there are many levels. This is a disadvantage that should be remembered when opting for a narrow span of control. It will also take a long time for a man to climb many rungs in the promotion ladder. However, a flat organization has the disadvantage that that there are less opportunities for promotion, since there are fewer tiers in the hierarchy.

We have seen that facilitating co-ordination is an important criterion in grouping. The problem of achieving good co-ordination is such a difficult one that the next chapter is devoted to it.

SUMMARY

Most managers will, at some time in their careers, have to decide how to group work, that is how best to combine the different activities for which they are responsible. Before they decide they should be clear what are the alternatives. The different forms of grouping are: products or services (sometimes called 'purpose'); functions (sometimes called 'process'); customers, place and time. Most organizations include a number of different types of grouping with one as the primary division, and the others as subsidiary.

What is the most suitable form of grouping for the situation must be determined by weighing up the merits and drawbacks of the possible alternatives. There are a number of criteria that can be used for doing so. It will be desirable to try to minimize problems of co-ordination, but doing so may conflict with the need to take advantage of specialization. In general, the larger the organization the more important does it become to try to facilitate co-ordination. The relative economics of different forms of grouping should obviously be considered. The grouping should, as far as possible, avoid ambiguity about the work to be done, and about who should do it, though there can also be dangers in being too precise. Some forms of groupings are much more likely than others to generate conflict between individuals and groups, so the avoidance of conflict is another criterion. In some organizations an adequate understanding of local conditions will also be valuable. The relative importance of these different criteria will depend upon the aims of the organization.

Divisionalization has become popular in some large organizations in an attempt to create more manageable units. Each division may group its activities in a number of different ways. The main alternative to divisionalization is a functional organization. The latter remains popular with companies with particular characteristics, including those in some process industries.

The span of control (that is, the number of immediate subordinates reporting to a manager) is another type of decision that must be made in grouping activities. There are limits to the number of people one manager can effectively supervise. What these limits are depend on a variety of factors including the nature of the work, the extent to which the subordinates' work is interrelated, and how much training and experience they have had. Management policy must also affect the span of control. Does management favour tight control, or does it want to stimulate initiative? The former is an argument for a small span, the latter for a large one.

.   .   .

1. This is sometimes called 'grouping by purpose'. It is the preferable term when talking about non-industrial organizations. An example of organization by purpose in a hospital is the grouping together of a wide variety of activities under the hospital secretary, all of which are concerned with the purpose of feeding and housing the patient.

2. The word 'functions' is commonly used to refer to the main types of activity such as production or sales. It has been, perhaps optimistically, defined as 'any task involved in the performance of the activities of an enterprise that can be clearly distinguished from any other task'. (Elmore Petersen, E. Grosvenor Plowman and Joseph M. Trickett, *Business Organization and Management*, 5th edn (Homewood, Ill., 1962) p. 160.)

3. The classical writers called this 'grouping by process'. It was used in reference to public organizations. Applied to manufacturing industry it can cause confusion as grouping by process can refer to the different stages in manufacturing. Hence the term 'functions' is preferable for this type of grouping.

4. E. L. Trist and K. W. Bamforth, 'Some Social and Psychological Consequences of the Longwall Method of Coal Getting', *Human Relations*, vol. 4, no. 1 (1951) pp. 3–38.

5. A. K. Rice, *Productivity and Social Organization: The Ahmedabad Experiment* (London, Tavistock, 1958) p. 4.

6. Dale, *Organization*, p. 110.

7. For a discussion of studies of what companies actually do about the span of control see Rosemary Stewart, *The Reality of Management* (London, Heinemann, 1963) pp. 31–4; (paperback edn, Pan, 1967) pp. 41–3.

8. L. Urwick, *The Elements of Administration,* 2nd edn (London, Pitman, 1947) pp. 52–3.

4 Co-ordination: Problems and Remedies

We are all familiar with stories about how one part of an organization failed to co-ordinate with another, like the government department that sold surplus goods to a merchant who made a large profit selling them to another government department. Such stories are told for laughs. To the layman they are ludicrous follies, but the manager, whether in private or public organizations knows how hard it can be to keep departments adequately informed of each other's activities and needs.

When people work on related activities what they do must be co-ordinated so that it contributes most efficiently to the common purpose. To do this is one of the most important and difficult problems of organization. This chapter will look at why there are co-ordination problems, and will discuss the different methods that can be used to tackle them.

In an ideal organization co-ordination would be a task, but not a problem. All members would will the good of the organization, that is they would agree on what was their common purpose and would work together to achieve it. They would be more interested in pursuing the objectives of the organization than in their own individual or departmental interests. They would actively and intelligently seek to ensure that what they did contributed to the efficiency of the whole. They would also be perfectly informed about the effects of their activities on other departments. Such a description, as we all know, does not correspond to any man-made organization. Hence where there is a need for co-ordination there is always a problem in trying to achieve it.

The description of what would happen in an ideal organization provides a guide to what can be done to reduce problems of co-ordination. First, members of the organization should know and agree on their common objective. This statement may be too idealistic, but at least it points to the value of defining organizational goals and of trying to ensure that these are widely known and understood. It also means that managers should be encouraged to think in terms of the good of the organization rather than purely that of their own department or division. In the ideal organization we said that members would be perfectly informed of the effects of their activities on other departments. Again, this is difficult to achieve, but much can be done to make it easier. Later in this chapter we shall be discussing ways of improving co-ordination, but first it will be useful to look at some particular problems of co-ordination.

WHY PROBLEMS ARISE
Co-ordination problems can arise because people do not know what they should be doing to relate their activities to those of other parts of the organization. They can be created by bad work allocation and by poor grouping of activities. The most difficult to deal with are the problems that stem from conflicts of interest. These may be between individuals, between groups or departments, and between the organization as a whole and its constit-

uent parts. This section will be mainly concerned with problems of this kind. The next, which discusses remedies, will deal with all types of co-ordination problems.

Organizational v. local interests

A conflict of interest exists when the profitability of a subsidiary company is greater if it does one thing, but the profit of the company as a whole is greater if the subsidiary does something else. The conflict is increased when the subsidiary is treated as a profit centre and the efficiency of its top management is assessed by the local profits, which may even be the basis for bonus payments. Group services, such as transport, which have to be paid for by those who use them, often result in such a clash of interests. It may be cheaper for the subsidiary company or division to buy the services outside, but if allowance is made for the contribution to overheads it may be more economical for the company as a whole if group services are used.

The extent to which the activities of subsidiary companies, or separate divisions, in a large organization need to be co-ordinated will depend upon company policy. At one extreme of centralization the directors may seek to ensure common policies throughout the organization for all aspects of the business. At the other, the directors of the parent company may only set profitability criteria and make the top appointment(s), otherwise each subsidiary will be free to act as an independent company. The latter policy is unusual, the directors of most large organizations do establish some common policies. Such policies will not necessarily create a need for co-ordination, or a conflict of interest. The need for co-ordination, and possibly for a more centralized policy, arises, for example, when the wages and conditions offered by one part of the company are used as an argument by the unions for demanding similar conditions elsewhere. Where this happens local management must ask themselves what will be the repercussions of what they do elsewhere in the organization. There may for them be a conflict of interest, at least in the short term, between the agreement that they wish to conclude with the unions and what would be best for the organization as a whole. The danger that local management may put their own interests before that of the group as a whole may lead top management to adopt a more centralized industrial relations policy.

Conflicts between departments

The conflict of interest between sales and production is a continuing problem in many manufacturing companies. It will, of course, be much reduced if the sales and works managers are genuinely more interested in the company's good than in that of their own department. Then there will not be a conflict of interest, but there may still be a wide difference in viewpoint, stemming from the special needs and problems of their departments. Production wants a steady and predictable rate of production so that they can plan to use their resources of men and machinery as efficiently as possible. They will also want to produce as few varieties of products as possible so as to permit longer runs.

The sales department wants to attract and please customers by providing the variations that they ask for and by supplying goods whenever they are requested. Sales may make promises to customers about deliveries without consulting the works to see if they can be kept. Nor is this failure likely to be purely a question of insufficient information about the works' position. Sales may argue— as one can hear them doing in management meetings of very different types of companies—'If we ask production they will say "No", but if we don't they will manage somehow.' The reverse happens too. Sales complain that they were not consulted about the quantities that they could sell before the works produced them. Production may retort: 'If we have produced the stuff they will have to sell it. We have found from experience that they can sell more under pressure than they will admit to in advance.' Both sides may have discovered that they can successfully put pressure on the other in that way. This discovery, and consequent tactics, can become self-defeating if the other department starts to protect itself by saying that it can do less than it anticipates.

The conflict of interests that often arises between production and sales is one illustration of the co-ordination problems that can result from such differences. It was chosen as it is one of the commonest and best known, but there are many others. In hospitals there are frequent complaints by nursing and administrative staff of consultants' failures to co-ordinate their activities with those of other people. Here the problem is that individual consultants may act without thinking of the organizational repercussions of what they do.

Competition for services

The typing pool, in itself a fairly simple work unit, can illustrate many of the conflicts of interest that arise when people are competing for scarce resources.

A well-run typing pool should try and ensure as even a flow of work as possible so that the typists are not hopelessly overburdened at one period, with long delays for the customers, and with little to do at other times. There is also a need to try to assess priorities at times of pressure so that the most urgent work gets typed first. Users of typing pools are likely to make these tasks difficult. Many of them will think that their work must have priority. Few will have the foresight to warn the typing pool that they have a large job coming up. The problems for the typing pool are likely to be complicated by the fact that those asking for services may have different pulling power. Differences due to official status can easily be accommodated. It is usually the most senior person who will get his work done first. There will also be unofficial differences in pulling power, due to friendship or even fear. One man may get preference because he is so nice, or because he is an old buddy, another may get preference because if he does not he makes himself unpleasant—though this form of pressure may produce the opposite effect. The usual way of trying to minimize co-ordination difficulties is to make the typing pool supervisor responsible for dealing with all requests for typing and for allocation of work. This ensures that one person is responsible for co-ordination. She is able to assess the overall load on the unit. She is also in a better position to resist pressures than the individual typist.

Failures in communication

Co-ordination problems are often attributed to bad information. It may be a correct explanation, but it can be an excuse for poor management attitudes. A good communications system is no substitute for a willingness to co-operate with other managers. Hence the need to be aware of sources of conflicts of interest and of the reasons for differences in viewpoint. This is not to underrate the importance of a good communications system.

Many co-ordination problems arise because people do not know how their activities are affecting other people who should be kept informed or even consulted before action is taken. This is most likely to be true in times of change unless planning has tried to foresee the areas where co-ordination will be needed, and has done so correctly. Here planning techniques such as critical path analysis can be helpful. Planning will need to consider both the content of the information that different departments and sections may need if they are to keep their activities in step, and also its timing; that is, when the information will be needed. What, for instance, does the marketing department need to know about the new product and when does it need to know it if it is to plan the marketing effectively? Public relations officers are much concerned with ensuring that reporters get the right information—from the organization's viewpoint—and get it at the right time. The press release is a simple device for trying to co-ordinate the release of news.

REDUCING THE PROBLEM

Good organization can help to reduce both the need for, and the problems of, co-ordination, but the methods that are appropriate in one organization may not be suitable in another where conditions are different.

Joan Woodward has suggested, in her study of the relationship between the organization of firms and their technology, that companies that produce one-offs or small batches need to have a much closer day-to-day relationship between marketing, development and production than do firms in process industries or in large-batch and mass-production.[1] This means that in the former there must be much closer co-ordination, achieved mainly through discussions. In the other two groups of companies less co-ordination is needed and more can be achieved by written exchange of information.

Organizations undergoing a rapid rate of change will tend to have more co-ordination problems than those that are experiencing little change. Those in a relatively stable environment should have learnt where co-ordination is necessary and what should be done to achieve it. Those with a rapid rate of change will have to give more attention to promoting it and to trying to foresee the new co-ordination needs that will arise. Co-ordination must be an on-going activity if it is to keep up with changing conditions.

Chain of command

This is the main method that is used to co-ordinate the activities of different individuals and groups. Every manager who is in charge of subordinates who work on related activities must try and ensure that their work is co-ordinated. This will be one of his major responsibilities.

The value of a hierarchy in facilitating co-ordination has been shown in studies of both laboratory and normal organizations. Blau and Scott, reviewing laboratory studies of the effects on performance of the organization of small groups, concluded that 'hierarchical organization

serves important functions for achieving co-ordination and
that it does so specifically by restricting the free flow of
communication'.[2] If the groups are hierarchically organized—that is, they have a leader—he assumes the dominant
role of co-ordinator.

Kaufman, in his study of how the U.S. Forest Service
worked, concluded that 'Hierarchy . . . is certainly one
of the ways the Forest Service has avoided the splintering
effects of other characteristics of a large and complex
agency'.[3] After pointing out that the Ranger (he is the
manager in charge of a forest district) issues all instructions to his subordinates and that all superiors must go
through him, Kaufman described the advantages of the
chain of command as follows:

> The existence, at each level, of a single, determinate in-
> dividual formally empowered to issue decisions with respect
> to all functions—decisions not subject to further appeal at
> the same level—means that the competing claims of the
> several functional specialties will often be judged in terms
> of more general criteria of decision. It also relieves higher
> headquarters of torrents of detail from below that would
> otherwise impede concentration on the full-time task of
> maintaining integration. At the same time, it safeguards
> field units against incessant intervention by functional spe-
> cialists from above, unco-ordinated intervention that could
> result in hopeless confusion in the field. And it cuts down
> the problems of communication by establishing, close to
> the field, 'switchboards' in which general directives are
> adapted to the specific conditions of limited areas, and in
> which inconsistencies are often discovered and eliminated
> before instructions take effect upon field personnel.[4]

Good grouping
The way in which activities are grouped can help to

reduce the amount of co-ordination that is necessary and can make it easier to achieve. Unfortunately, there are, as we saw in the previous chapter, other criteria for grouping which may be considered more important than that of easing problems of co-ordination. Where this is so it is even more important to think about co-ordination needs. The manager should ask himself: 'Where are there likely to be co-ordination problems?' and 'What can I do to reduce them?' More simply, he can ask himself too: 'Who will need to talk to whom?' and 'What am I doing to make it easy for them to do so?'

Committees

Grumbling about the time spent in committees is a favourite managerial pastime in some companies. This is more likely to be a reflection on the way the committees work, or rather fail to work, than a necessary condemnation of committees as such. Many may feel sympathy at times with the man who said, 'The ideal committee consists of three people, with two people absent', but would still admit, perhaps with regret, that committees are often a necessary means of co-ordination.

A study made in 1960 in the United States, of a cross-section of managers in companies of different sizes, showed that 81 per cent said that their organizations had regular committees, but only 8 per cent would have liked to abolish them.[5] Nearly all these executives saw committees as a necessary part of management. They said that their greatest advantage was in facilitating interdepartmental co-ordination. They also valued them as the best way to ensure informed decisions and because they promoted creativity through the exchange of ideas. Top management made more favourable remarks about committees and fewer unfavourable ones than middle management. Junior management were the most critical. Unfortunately the study gives no indications of the reasons for these differences of viewpoint. One may be that at the more senior management levels decisions are longer-term and more uncertain and therefore are more suited to committee deliberations.

The study by the author into how 160 middle and senior managers, in a wide variety of companies, spent their time for a month showed that the average amount of time spent in committee was about three hours a week, but that an average was misleading as one in seven of the managers spent no time in committee.[6] The amount of time spent in committees varied considerably even in companies of the same size.

Committees, though they are a useful and, sometimes, an indispensable means of co-ordination, can easily be abused. They may be set up unnecessarily. They are highly likely to continue to meet after the need for them has passed. They are difficult to run efficiently. Hence the value of looking critically at all proposals for new committees to decide whether they can serve a useful purpose and, of reviewing at intervals, whether existing committees are still needed.

The advantages of committees are a guide to when they can be helpful. These are:

1. *They can improve decision-making by bringing together all those whose experience is necessary to the decision.*

They are a means of co-ordinating the different viewpoints and knowledge of departments, and so ensuring that no relevant knowledge is overlooked. It is easier to judge how strongly people feel about particular points in a group discussion than in written memoranda.

2. *They can prevent decisions being taken too quickly.*

Most people would think that a committee's capacity to delay decision-taking is one of its great disadvantages, but there can be times when it is important to try and reach the best decision, even if this takes longer, and where this can best be done in a committee, rather than in an informal group.

3. *Committees can have an educational value in keeping managers informed about the work of other parts of the company,* but the use of committees purely for information purposes should be treated with caution, as there may be less time-consuming ways of achieving the same thing. In one company, where the managers kept diaries for the author of their activities and answered daily questions about the use of their time, there were many complaints from middle managers about the amount of time wasted in large committees. Top managers described what a useful committee system they had—such a convenient method of keeping managers informed. They thought of committee meetings for information as a way of saving their time, but did not appreciate what a waste of time these meetings seemed to the middle managers.

4. *Decisions made by committees are likely to be more objective than those made by an individual* as there is more chance of preconceived ideas and emotional judgements being examined.

The advantages of committees have been discussed

first, because managers are probably aware of their disadvantages. These can be summed up briefly as:

1. They can slow down action, or even stifle it altogether, thus inhibiting innovation.

2. They weaken accountability because no one may feel responsible for a decision taken by a committee.

3. They take the time of a number of people both in the actual meetings and in the paperwork before and after. For some, or all, of the people present at least part of the meeting may be a waste of time.

A minor drawback is that it can be very difficult to find a date that suits all, or even many, of the members of the committee.

What can be done to try and make the time spent in committees more profitable? Dale has usefully summed up some of the lessons from research and writing as:

1. (a) Composition: members should have homogeneity of outlook so that they may be able to reach agreement, but heterogeneity of background so that each can make a distinctive contribution to the discussion.

   (b) Strong personality clashes should be avoided as they are likely to inhibit constructive discussion.

   (c) Ideally members should want to take a moderate part in the discussion, being neither too active nor too retiring. However, there may be good reasons for not aiming at the ideal as it might mean excluding an overly talkative character who yet had an original contribution to make.

2. Subject-matter: two groups of subjects are specially suitable for committees:

   (a) problems that have many possible solutions;

(*b*) those that affect many aspects of the organization.
3. Size: the size that is appropriate will obviously vary with the purpose of the committee. Smaller groups are better for reaching conclusions. Bales, after experimental studies of small groups, has suggested that committees should be limited to seven members.[7]

Whatever the composition, size and purpose of the committee, good chairmanship will make a great difference to the speed and usefulness of the discussion. Efficient preparation of committee papers can also make a useful contribution.

Informal discussions

Much co-ordination takes place in informal discussions, often among managers at the same level but in different departments. These discussions may happen only as the need arises, or they may become so much part of the way the organization works that they should be described as informal organization. Such horizontal contacts have the advantage of causing few or no status problems, hence the people involved are likely to talk more freely to each other than to people of a different rank from themselves. In many organizations it is desirable that such discussions take place at all levels in the management hierarchy.

The value of facilitating informal contacts between those whose work is related is often forgotten by those who plan office layouts. People are most likely to talk with those that they meet naturally, whether in a communal office, restaurant, lift, lavatory or corridor. They will tend to feel friendly to them, as studies have shown that propinquity intensifies people's feelings for each other and that they more often like than dislike each other.

The value of managers' dining-rooms is often recognized in companies as a means of facilitating contact, as well as a mark of status. Even those who dislike the creation of separate dining-rooms for the latter reason may yet think that it is worth while for the former reason. But who is it most useful that people should talk to at lunch-time? This is something that the builders of new hospitals should think about. In the older hospitals it is customary for matron to eat in the sisters' dining-room or at a separate table in the nurses' dining-room, the medical staff eat in a dining-room of their own, and the more senior administrative staff may go home to lunch or eat in a canteen which caters for the rest of the staff. This division of dining-rooms helps to perpetuate the distinctions between nursing, medical and administrative.

Mid-morning coffee or afternoon tea is the recognized time in some academic and research institutions when people from different departments meet together. Inter-departmental queries tend to be raised then. It is convenient to do so, because one knows that that is when one can expect to see the man you want to talk to and because it avoids interrupting his work at other times. In hospitals the hospital secretary and matron may make a practice of taking coffee together so that they can discuss any common problems. Such informal get-togethers provide the opportunity to talk about related problems, but because they are informal they need only be used when needed and the time taken can be much more flexible than in formal meetings.

Projects

The establishment of a separate group is a method that is increasingly used to co-ordinate work on a new project. The staff, including the project manager, are often seconded from other departments to work together for the duration of the project. On its completion they will probably return to their old departments. The establishment of a separate group means that its members concentrate on the project for its duration. They become members of the same unit, instead of remaining members of different departments who are trying to work together on a common task, but who may be distracted by their departmental loyalties.

The separate project group can be a powerful tool for ensuring co-ordination between people of different backgrounds. It is most suitable where there is a clear job to be done, which has a definite end, and which can, therefore, provide a clear objective for members of the group. The composition of the group is important, especially if it is a small one. The members should be able to work together and should have different contributions to make.

The special co-ordinator

Some large companies have thought it necessary to create new posts with responsibilities for co-ordinating different aspects of the business. These posts are distinct from the co-ordinating functions of line managers as the jobs do not usually carry with them executive authority. The men who hold these posts are expected to achieve co-ordination by persuasion alone, rather than by persuasion backed by authority.

SUMMARY

Co-ordination is necessary to ensure that related activities in different groups and departments mesh together and contribute to the common purpose. Wherever there is a need for co-ordination there is likely to be a problem in obtaining it. Problems arise from the conflicts of interest between individuals, groups and departments, and between the organization as a whole and its subdivisions. Problems come too from the different viewpoints of those in dissimilar jobs. Then there are the difficulties caused by bad work allocation, poor grouping of activities and by inadequate communications.

Co-ordination problems can be reduced by good organization, but the most appropriate method will vary with the circumstances. An organization that is in a stable environment can have more formalized means of co-ordination than one that has to cope with rapid change, or with making a one-off product.

The main means of co-ordination is the chain of command. Each manager has to try and synchronize the work of those of his subordinates whose work is related. The way in which activities are grouped will have an important effect on the amount of co-ordination that is needed and on the ease or difficulty with which it can be achieved. Committees, despite their disadvantages, are a useful means of co-ordinating the knowledge and viewpoints of different individuals and departments. Anyone considering setting up a committee should be familiar with their uses and abuses and the ways in which they can be made to work best. Much co-ordination can be achieved by informal discussions and thought should be given to making it easy for the people who need to talk to each other to do so. Here the physical layout and the eating arrangements are particularly important. Finally, there are two other methods of co-ordination that are useful in some circumstances: the project group and the special co-ordinator.

. . .

1. Woodward, *Industrial Organization,* chap. 8.

2. Peter M. Blau and W. Richard Scott, *Formal Organizations* (London, Routledge & Kegan Paul, paperback edition, 1966) pp. 127–8.

3. Kaufman, *Forest Ranger,* p. 210.

4. Ibid.

5. R. Tillman Jr, 'Problems in Review: Committees on Trial', *Harvard Business Review* (Mar–Apr 1960) pp. 7–12, 162–72.

6. Rosemary Stewart, *Managers and their Jobs* (London, Macmillan, 1967) pp. 44–5.

7. Dale, *Organization,* pp. 175–6. Dale's report of Bales's work is taken from Robert Bales, 'In Conference', *Harvard Business Review* (Mar–Apr 1954) pp. 44–50.

PART III

SOME COMMON ORGANIZATIONAL PROBLEMS

The main problems that arise in organizations are of three kinds. There are those that stem from relationships between individuals and groups; those that arise from trying to keep a good balance between the advantages and disadvantages of different forms of organization; and those that result from changes affecting the organization.

Some types of relationships are potentially a problem in any kind of organization. There are the problems of relations between superiors and subordinates, where effective communications up and down are often difficult to achieve. There are the problems that arise between managers and specialists—this description is chosen instead of the more usual, and narrower, 'line and staff'. Finally, there are the problems that arise in relations within management, an area of organizational behaviour that research is gradually telling us more about. These three types of problems are discussed in separate chapters.

The most difficult problems that arise in medium- and large-scale organizations are those of striking a balance between different organizational policies. A fourth chapter is devoted to the problem of deciding what is the right balance between the need for control, an argument for centralization, and the need to encourage initiative, an argument for decentralization. A fifth chapter considers the conflict between the need for order and that for flexibility.

*The last two chapters consider different aspects of
the problems of change in organizations. The first discusses
what are the organizational problems of planning for
management succession. The second chapter, called
'The Changing Organization', seeks to relate changes
in the environment to the changes that have taken
place in organizations. Illustrations are given of the impact
of these changes on a large industrial company
and on a hospital group.*

5 Superior—Subordinate Relationships

This is a subject on which a great deal has been written and innumerable studies conducted. Much of the writing and research has focused on the first-line supervisor and his workers. Here the focus will be primarily on relations within management. This chapter aims to look briefly at the problems of the superior–subordinate relationship, to describe some of the things that research has revealed about it, and to discuss some of the ways in which the organization can help to determine the character of this relationship.

The superior–subordinate relationship is the main, sometimes the only, one that is formally established by the organization. It is the one that is shown on the traditional organization chart. For most managers it is a key relationship and takes up more time than any other type of contact.[1]

On the success of the relationship between the superior and his staff will largely depend the efficiency of his department. Not only is it important for the superior, but also for the subordinate, since it is likely to affect his future prospects as well as how he feels about his present job.

HOW THE SETTING AFFECTS THE RELATIONSHIP

The cultural background

The relationship between a superior and a subordinate does not exist in a vacuum, but in a particular cultural and organizational setting which helps to determine its character. The culture of the country, perhaps even of the locality, provides the stage for the two roles. The degree of formality or of camaraderie between the two will be influenced by the cultural pattern, and so will be the type of leadership. In some countries the manager will be expected to be autocratic, in others a more democratic, participative approach will be the custom especially at the managerial level. A Japanese subordinate would be expected to be more deferential to his boss than would an American or a Britisher. In China, for some years, managers have had to spend two to three days a week in manual work. The aim is to keep them in close touch with the workers so that there is no gulf in understanding. Unfortunately for Western sociologists, none is likely to be in a position to judge what effect the doctrine of manual work for managers has had on the superior–subordinate relationship.

The differences in cultural background of different countries can provide hazards for the expatriate manager. In an Asian country for example, the newly appointed English-factory manager wanted to establish friendly relations with his work-force. On one of his factory inspections he stopped to talk with one of the girls and to say something nice about her work. He chose one of the plainest girls, so that his action should not be misinterpreted. When he was leaving the factory at the end of the day he was stopped by a seedy-looking man, who said: 'You like my sister. How much?'

The organizational setting

The national culture sets the general expectations that people have of the relationship between superior and subordinates, within this there can be variations caused by the traditions that have grown up in the organization, the nature of the formal organization and the personalities of the individuals. The formal organization can affect the relationship in two main ways. The first is by the span of control that it establishes. If the manager has many subordinates he will not be able to supervise their work as closely as he can when he has only a few. The second way in which the formal organization can affect the relationship is by the amount of support that it gives to the manager's formal authority. The managers may be given certain powers over their subordinates such as the right to hire and fire and to determine, within limits, pay increases. There may also be marks of rank and status that distinguish each level in the hierarchy.

How far should the organization seek to support the formal authority of its managers? The most powerful weapon that it can give the manager is the right to hire and fire and many managers and foremen deplore the fact that they no longer have this right, though some are able to recommend that an employee should be sacked. Often even the organization no longer has the power to do so because of union restrictions. In the Civil Service once an employee has become established he can only be

sacked for gross misdemeanours. Even where there are
no specific union restrictions personnel policies are usually opposed to giving a manager the sole right of dis-
charge. Managers in many organizations, therefore, have
to get on without the power of the sack. In times of full
employment it may not be much of a deterrent, even
when they have it.

How useful is the other type of support for formal
authority, that of marks of rank and status? The marks
of rank, whether they be uniforms or the use of a title
or a surname, help to create social distance between the
levels in the hierarchy, so does the use of separate dining-
rooms and lavatories. Social distance means that the relations between levels are likely to be more formal and that
the manager is likely to be treated with the outward
marks of respect. Some managers are afraid that without
these formal signs of respect their authority will be under-
mined. Whether the manager does in practice lose any of
his power of control over his subordinates depends upon
his ability to exercise personal authority or influence. A
man who has nothing in himself to earn the respect and
co-operation of his staff will be powerless without the
formal authority of his position. Even with it his ability
to control subordinates will be very limited—in reality
they have some power too, if only that of passive resist-
ance. One unpopular manager worked himself almost
into the grave as his subordinates always did what he
asked them to do and never did anything else; an ingenious and very effective form of working to rule. The more
a manager needs the co-operation of his staff—and the
more skilled and interrelated the work the more he will
need it—the less he can rely on formal authority to obtain

it. Social distance can be a handicap as it may impede a free give-and-take of information.

The reader who visits other organizations might try observing the relations between superiors and subordinates. How much social distance is there between them? What does he think is the explanation for differences between two organizations? How far does he think it is due to differences in the work or to the influence of tradition, or to particular personalities? There are many ways of establishing social distance which he can notice, apart from formal provisions by the organization such as separate lavatories. Does the subordinate get up when his superior comes into the room? Does he sit down in his superior's room without being invited to do so? Is he introduced to callers and how is the introduction made? Are christian names used? If so, when and by whom? If he is observant he will notice these and many other examples.

The organization can have other influences upon the relationship between superior and subordinate apart from those that are formally established. Kahn and his colleagues in the United States suggest that there are five types of organizational behaviour that seem to be characteristic of the organization rather than of particular individuals or jobs. These are:

> the extent to which the individual is expected to obey rules and follow orders;
> the extent to which superiors are expected to show a personal interest in and to nurture their subordinates;
> the extent to which all relationships are conducted according to general rather than individual standards;
> how detailed supervision is expected to be:
> the extent to which organization members are expected to strive actively for achievement and advancement.[2]

This list shows how considerable can be the influence of the organization on the relationship between superiors and subordinates.

PROBLEMS OF THE RELATIONSHIP

1. *From the superior's point of view*

The superior has to decide how he should divide the work between himself and his subordinates. This means that he must decide what he should delegate and to whom. Delegation has three aspects to it. First is the assigning of tasks to particular subordinates. Next is giving them the authority to carry out these tasks, which includes the means for doing so, and last is making them responsible for those tasks. Although the manager should hold his subordinate responsible for the work he has delegated he does not lessen his own responsibility for the efficiency of his command.

The manager's main problem, though he may not realize it, is in knowing what he should do himself. He should first decide what are the things he should do because of his position. The fact that he is at a particular level in the hierarchy, whether it is at the top or lower down, means that there are special advantages of his position that he should use. He will have more power than his subordinates and this can be important for some types of contact. He will also have a representative role for his group, as managing director for his company, or as a departmental head for his department, and so there will be some jobs that he alone should do. He also needs to concern himself with the more important policy decisions affecting his

command, and not be so preoccupied with day-to-day matters that he does not have time for this. He should create
and maintain a climate that encourages his subordinates
to work well. Finally, he must retain the overall responsibility for checking on the work of his command. These
are the jobs he should do because of his position in the
hierarchy. There may be other tasks that he thinks that
he can do better than his staff. Such a decision is fraught
with the dangers of self-deception and the wish to continue doing work that one enjoys rather than what may
be the less congenial, but more appropriate, work for
that position.

The manager should remember that although he can
more easily get information from the managers at his own
level than his subordinates, they may more readily get
information from their peers. In a large organization interdepartmental relations may be much franker among junior managers than they are higher up. So the manager
should recognize that his staff may be in a better position to find out what is happening than he is.

Once he has decided what he ought to be doing, and
what work he should delegate to his subordinates, he can
turn to the problem of how to divide the delegated work
amongst them. He may be influenced by the classical writers who talk of equating authority and responsibility, but
this implies that the work can be divided into neat par-
cels, one for each job. In practice, the work may be such
that it will be done best if his staff act as a team. Even
if the work can be parcelled out he may think that it is
undesirably restrictive to give his staff specifically defined
responsibilities. Sometimes he may not understand enough
about his subordinates' work to do so, even if he wanted

to. This may well be the position of a manager who is responsible for a new type of specialist, or one who has subordinates trained in a different discipline from his own.

Next the manager must be able to communicate what he wants done to his staff, as well as being willing to listen and able to understand what it is they say about the work.[3] The first essential to explaining what one wants done— and this is where many managers fail—is in being sufficiently clear in one's own mind about what one wants. The manager should make it clear to his subordinates what he expects of them. How far he should spell out these expectations will depend in part upon the stability of the work that has to be done and in part upon the ability and experience of his staff. New or poorly trained staff will need more detail than those who are experienced. In a stable situation the superior should be able to describe clearly what are the objectives, how they should be achieved and how their achievement should be measured. In more fluid situations a group exploration of what needs doing and of how to do it may be more fruitful than prescriptions from the superior.

The manager must know whether he and his staff speak a common language, as those with a common professional training should do, or whether he must make allowances for misunderstanding that can arise from different backgrounds. A more difficult barrier to communications stems from the superior–subordinate relationship itself. Each is likely to tell the other what he wants to communicate rather than what the other wants to hear. Some superiors can inspire sufficient confidence to greatly reduce this barrier, but few are likely to overcome it altogether.

A traditional task of the manager is 'motivation', now more fashionably called 'leadership style', that of getting people to do what he wants. Leavitt distinguishes three main ways of doing so: by the use of formal authority, by manipulation, and by influence.[4] He suggests that a superior who relies on his formal authority is narrowing his effective range of control over others. He discusses the pros and cons of using authority. The advantages of using authority are that it imposes orderliness and conformity. This simplifies the problems of co-ordination and control. It is simpler to use authority, because it is generally understood, whereas if one wants to use persuasion one must understand the motivations of the individual one is seeking to persuade. Authority is faster, as time is not taken by explanations. Finally, some people enjoy exercising authority and like the demonstrations of respect that it may produce. The disadvantages of using authority are that: it may produce unintended reactions, such as a show of conformity without the reality, and an atmosphere of distrust and hostility; also it may reduce the possibilities of future communication and hence the superior's opportunity to influence the subordinate—Leavitt calls this the 'irreversibility of restrictive methods'. In general, he suggests that formal authority is more used, and more useful, at the lower levels of the pyramid. At the managerial level it is a change of attitude rather than of actions that is wanted, and this is more likely to be achieved by influence than by exercising formal authority.

Finally, the manager must check to see that what he wanted done has been done. This raises problems of what methods to use, how technically efficient they are, and how they will be seen by his staff. At one extreme, his staff may view his attempts at control as imposed and unreasonable; to be circumvented, whenever possible. At the other extreme, they may view them as targets that they suggested and that have been mutually agreed and reviewed.

Management-by-objectives is now the fashionable answer to how to provide an acceptable framework for control. Like all fashions in management it has its dangers that too much will be expected from it, but it is a method that focuses attention on, and provides a logical framework for, assessing achievement. The idea of management by objectives is, of course, not a new one, what is being advocated is a more formalized method of identifying and defining goals and targets. An essential part is the interpretation and communication of objectives for personnel at all levels.

We have looked at the traditional problems of the superior in his relations with his staff. The problem areas have remained the same, but the character of the relationship has changed. Circumstances have made the boss a less authoritarian figure than in the past. Full employment has made him more interested in keeping his staff, sometimes even afraid that they might leave. The higher level of education and the more democratic character of society have made an autocratic manner old-fashioned. The decreasing value in many organizations of experience compared with up-to-date knowledge has reduced the superior's authority. He is less likely to be able to dictate what ought to be done, instead he may have to ask his subordinate's advice as to what should be done. The older manager may well be a rather worried and insecure person as he hears his staff talking about things that he does not understand. Hence some of the costly top-management appreciation courses that try to meet his need to bring himself up to date.

A further problem for some superiors is that they are too anxious to be liked by their staff—a characteristic of some British managers, but not of many of their European neighbours, who are more interested in being respected. This anxiety may make some British managers reluctant to criticize, for fear their subordinate may resent it. The superior's job can be a lonely one, though this is truest for the man at the top and for those on the first rung. The former can be in an isolated position with no peers in his own organization. The latter will, if he is promoted from the shop floor, have lost the camaraderie of his work-mates without becoming a real member of the management team.

2. *From the subordinate's point of view*

The superior may feel that the problems are all on his side, but that is not how many subordinates would see the relationship. Today, especially, the answers of many to the question 'What problems are there in your work?' would include 'educating the chief' or 'getting him to change his out-of-date approach'. This feeling, a common one for younger people to have about their elders, is intensified by the rapid rate of change which tends to date the superior more quickly than in the past. The subordinate's attitude to his superior is likely to be an ambivalent one. He may enjoy dependence, as most people do. He feels relieved to have somebody else whose job it is to cope in a crisis and who takes the final rap. He is also likely to resent the relationship, especially if he feels that he is working for somebody whom he thinks is incompetent or out of date. Of course, he may still resent the mere fact of being subordinate even where he respects his superior.

Another of the subordinate's problems is to please his chief. According to American research most managers, at least in the United States, tend to be upward-oriented. They care more about what their superior thinks of them than they do about what their subordinates think of them.

The superior is important for the subordinate's future, as it is his judgement of the subordinate's abilities that is most likely to affect the latter's promotion—even though companies with well-planned management development schemes may try to get other people to appraise too. The man who works for a powerful manager is likely to do best provided his manager approves of him, and does not selfishly try to keep him in his present job.

Subordinates often complain that they cannot please their manager because they do not know what he wants. This can happen because the superior does not know himself what he wants, or because he has not explained it clearly.

The discussion so far has assumed that the subordinate has only one superior. But he may have, as we shall discuss in the next chapter, both a line superior to whom he is ultimately responsible and a staff one to whom he is responsible for his professional standards. He may also be given instructions by his superior's superior and come into contact with others who are senior to him and whose requests he may feel it impolitic to refuse. He may therefore have multiple relationships with more senior managers. These can be stressful, particularly if the instructions and requests are at variance with those of his immediate superior. However, the ambitious man may welcome the opportunity to be visible to other senior managers.

LEADERSHIP STYLE

The title describes a central preoccupation of the human relations school, particularly in the United States, where many research workers have explored how performance is affected by the way a person leads. This was not a subject that interested the classical school of management writers. Although they described motivation as one of the tasks of management, they did not ask themselves research-type questions like 'what happens if the boss is autocratic?' or 'what is the effect of a manager who encourages his staff to participate in decision-making?'

What has research shown about the effectiveness of different styles of leadership? The main centre of this investigation from 1947 on was at the Institute of Social Research at the University of Michigan in the United States, under the leadership of Rensis Likert. The findings, from a study of a wide variety of different types of large organizations, showed that the best performance is obtained by leadership that is employee-centred. This means that the leader thinks first of the employee's welfare and only second of production, and that he supervises in a general rather than in a close, detailed way.[5] Such findings encouraged some of the members of the human relations school in the United States to urge the value of participative management, two-way communication and permissive leadership.

The universal applicability of these findings has since been questioned by a number of other studies, which show that the leadership style should vary with the situation and with the people concerned. Now many writers believe that there is no one best leadership style. What is best will depend on the circumstances, and these may vary in different parts of the organization as well as from one organization to another. In some organizations, or parts of the organization, initiative will be important, in others the punctual performance of prescribed duties may be what matters. For example, the research and development department, where the need is for innovation, seems to require a participative and egalitarian leadership style. This contrasts with the work of the production department where the greater need for short-term results requires a more directive style of leadership.

One reason for this change of approach amongst writers on leadership style is a greater recognition of the complexity of human motivation and of the variety of organizational situations. The question that the research workers who compared democratic and authoritarian styles of leadership were trying to answer was: 'What style of leadership do people respond to best?' Later research showed that there was no universal prescription. The indications are that various answers may be appropriate. Different men may have different needs (and women too); for example, some have a greater desire for dependence or initiative than others. Some leaders are naturally permissive, others naturally directive. The organizational needs will vary too.

What should be cheering to the manager is that observation shows that many different styles of leadership work. One may be preferable to another in a particular setting, but if it is alien to the manager's personality he is unlikely to make a better leader by radically trying to change his style.

A British study, by Sadler, showed the importance of an identifiable style. A study in two companies operating in a young and progressive industry showed that most people preferred a consultative style of leadership, but also that 'leaders who are seen as having distinct and identifiable styles of leadership are more effective in promoting confidence and satisfaction, *whatever style they adopt,* than those who do not have a distinctive style.' Sadler concluded: 'This suggests that one important characteristic of the successful leader is consistency of behaviour, which enable subordinates to know where they stand with him and to predict his actions and reactions.'[6]

SUMMARY

The main focus of the chapter is on supervisory relations within management.

The superior–subordinate relationship is formally established by the organization. For most managers it takes up more time than any other form of contact. It is a vital relationship for both parties.

The relationship is affected by its cultural and organizational setting, which sets the general expectation of behaviour. The formal organization influences the relationship by the span of control that it establishes and by the amount of support that it gives to the manager's formal authority. The marks of rank and status established by the formal organization create a social distance between the two. This increases manager's formal authority, but is liable to impede the free flow of information. Kahn and his colleagues have described other ways in which the organization may influence the relationship and have shown how considerable that influence can be.

The problems of the relationship were looked at first from the point of view of the superior and then from that of his subordinate. The superior must decide what work he should do himself and what he should delegate. He has to motivate his staff to do what he wants. He can do so by using his authority, by manipulation and by influence. He can provide the framework for assessing achievement by establishing agreed objectives. The subordinate is likely to have ambivalent feelings about his boss. One of his problems may be trying to educate him, and another may be trying to please him.

Much human relations research in the United States has studied the effects of different styles of leadership. The earlier research showed that the best performance is obtained by employee-centred leadership, and by a general rather than a close, detailed supervision. Later research indicated that there is no one best style. What is best in a particular instance will depend upon the nature of the work and upon the needs of the people being supervised. But, according to one English study, it is important for a leader to have a recognizable style so that his subordinates know where they stand with him.

• • •

1. The author's study of how 160 managers spent their time showed that on average two-thirds of their working time was spent

talking with other people. Eight per cent of their total working time was spent with their boss and 26 per cent with their subordinates. (*Managers and their Jobs*, pp. 57 and 59.)

2. R. L. Kahn and others, *Organizational Stress: Studies in Role Conflict and Ambiguity* (New York, Wiley, 1964). Quoted in D. Katz and R. L. Kahn, *The Social Psychology of Organizations* (New York, Wiley, 1964) p. 192.

3. The problems of communications, and the barriers that there are to it, are discussed in many books. Harold J. Leavitt has a useful discussion in *Managerial Psychology*, chap. 9.

4. Ibid., chap. 10, has a helpful discussion on how to influence behaviour.

5. Rensis Likert, *New Patterns of Management* (New York, McGraw-Hill, 1961).

6. P. J. Sadler, *Leadership Style, Confidence in Management and Job Satisfaction* (Ashridge Management College, Papers in Management Studies, May 1966) p. 16.

6 The Manager and the Specialist

Traditionally books on organization have a chapter on Line and Staff. Today this is too simple a distinction to cover all the different kinds of relationships that can exist between managers and specialists and the varying problems that may arise. Managers have to deal with an ever-increasing number of specialities which develop out of new technology, such as the computer, or which, as the result of increasing complexity, are hived off from the manager's job, such as long-range planning staffs. Managers stand in many different kinds of relationship to these varied specialists. Large organizations have a wide array of specialists, but small organizations are also likely to need some specialist help. The aim of this chapter is to look at these relationships, to analyse the kind of problems that arise, and to discuss what can be done to try and reduce them.

The phrase 'line and staff' often causes confusion because it is used in different ways by different writers. It is most often used to distinguish between the departments called 'line', where the managers contribute directly to the objectives of the organization either by producing a product or service or by selling it, and those departments, called 'staff' which contribute indirectly to promoting the objectives. Production and sales would, therefore, always be called 'line' in manufacturing companies. In some companies research and development, and in others finance, would also be considered line. In hospitals, medical and nursing are clearly 'line' activities. Some writers argue that it is difficult and misleading to try and distinguish between the activities of different departments in terms of which contribute directly to the organization's objectives, and which only facilitate, or contribute, indirectly. They say that the distinction should instead be based on the authority relationships as 'line tells, staff sells'. This distinction, too, has its difficulties as staff often do more than sell, they may also have some authority to tell other departments what to do. A similar but clearer distinction is that 'it is accountability for results that determine where the line authority resides'.[1] It should be remembered that whether the distinction between line and staff is based on activities or on accountability, the relationships within a staff department are line, that is the superior *tells* his subordinates and is accountable for their work, although he *sells* to other departments.

DIFFERENT ORGANIZATIONAL RELATIONSHIPS
BETWEEN MANAGERS AND SPECIALISTS

The nature of the problems that arise between managers and specialists vary with their organizational relationships. The specialist may be:

1. On the staff of the manager, and with no other organizational link.

2. On the staff of the manager, but with a functional relationship to a more senior member of his speciality.

3. In a separate department. These departments can

be distinguished by the nature of their relationship with the other departments:

(*a*) They are purely service departments.

(*b*) Their task is solely to advise management.

(*c*) They have some authority to determine policy as well to advise.

(*d*) They audit or inspect the work of other departments.

4. The specialist is outside the organization and is employed as a consultant.

The simplest relationship is the first one where the specialist is on the manager's staff and has no other organizational link. Such a relationship would not be discussed in a chapter that dealt only with problems of line and staff. Yet, even this relationship can be difficult, particularly for the older manager who has worked his way up from the bottom, and who is unused to the new specialty.

In the days when knowledge increased fairly slowly a manager would become more expert as a result of experience. Hence the manager was somebody who could be looked up to because he was likely to know best. The speeding up of technological change has altered this. Within the working lifetime of managers in many industries, especially those like steel and paper, which employed traditional skills, knowledge of the production process has greatly increased. It can be very galling to the older manager to find that his hard-won understanding of the process can be criticized by a much younger man with an academic training.

There are also new specialities, and much expansion and subdivision of old ones, which the manager may know little or nothing about. The old saying 'knowledge itself is power' applies to the organizational hierarchy, as subordinates who have specialist knowledge not shared by their bosses will have more power than colleagues whose training is in the same field as their boss. A chief accountant, for example, who has the computer manager reporting to him may find this a different type of relationship from that which he has with his accounting staff. It will depend, in part, on how much he understands of the computer manager's job.

The manager, therefore, has more and more to work with subordinates whose specialty he knows little or nothing about. This can create problems. They may arise partly from his own attitudes and those of his subordinates, but however good these attitudes are the manager still has the problem of how he can effectively manage something that he does not understand. The differences in attitude between managers and specialists will be discussed at a later stage. Here it is worth pointing out that the manager should not abdicate. He should train his staff to put forward their proposals in as simple a way as possible and to describe the nature of the choice in language he can understand. He should concern himself with the logic of their proposals and learn to ask questions that can help him, and them, to test this. In one company managers did not feel competent to ask questions about how a computer stock-control system was working. One day the works manager happened to notice that stocks of related nuts and bolts had got completely out of line. This story was told the author by a consultant who said 'Managers should not be afraid to ask common-sense questions.'

The second relationship, listed above, is where a specialist, such as a maintenance engineer, reports both to a man, usually called the line boss, who is responsible for what he does and when he does it, and also to a specialist superior outside the department, usually called the staff boss, who is responsible for how he does it. This is sometimes described as being 'administratively responsible' to the staff boss. The task of the staff boss is to maintain professional standards as he is in a position to judge professional competence. He may also lay down common procedures to be observed throughout the organization: the chief accountant may specify the form in which accounts are to be kept; the chief personnel officer may lay down policies for hiring and firing of employees; and the chief engineer may specify maintenance procedures.

The problems of the specialist reporting to a line manager, but also having what is called a 'functional' responsibility to a staff boss are obvious ones. They stem from the dual allegiance, from the possibility that the subordinate may be given conflicting instructions by his two bosses, and the likelihood that he may pay more attention to one boss than to the other, probably to the one that he thinks is most important in furthering his career. Problems are inevitable when a man has two bosses, but they can be increased or diminished by appropriate action and attitudes.

Important for the success of this relationship is the attitude of the three people. The subordinate should have integrity and not play one boss off against the other. The line and staff bosses should understand the demands of each other's work and seek to ensure that both contribute to the organization's objectives, instead of playing politics or thinking too narrowly in terms of their own department.

This description of desirable attitudes immediately shows how difficult it can be to achieve a satisfactory relationship. Important, too, is the organizational clarity of the relationship, so that the subordinate knows to whom he is responsible for what. In many companies subordinates do not know.

The third organizational relationship between the manager and the specialist is where the latter is in a separate department. These departments must be distinguished according to the tasks that they perform and the ways in which these impinge on the line manager. The simplest relationship with other departments is where the staff department provides a service that managers do not have to be persuaded to use. Catering is a good example; the typing pool is another, though this is more debatable as managers may prefer to have the typists within their own departments. The computer department can sometimes come in this category, where the users, such as engineers and research workers, regard it merely as a tool that provides a useful service. In these examples managers may grumble about the service that they get, but there will be none of the other difficulties that are found in relations between managers and specialists.

There are other types of specialist departments where the relationship between user and provider is more difficult. These are the departments providing a service, such as work-study or O. & M., which managers may not want to use, as they do the typing pool and the mail room. The department then has to sell its services, either literally in some companies, or in the sense of persuading managers to use them in others. The relationship between manager and specialist here is like that of some sellers and customers, with the former anxious to please and the latter perhaps sceptical perhaps concerned about how he can find out whether the service he is being offered is really worth while. The manager is unlikely to be perturbed by this type of relationship with the specialist, though, like any customer, there is always the danger that he may become disillusioned with what he has been sold. The specialist is more likely to have problems, as he may suffer from frustration if he feels that the value of his services is not recognized.

Specialists are most likely to feel frustrated in organizations where managers are not used to asking other departments for advice. Managers may feel threatened in such organizations if they are offered unsought advice. They may feel nervous at rejecting the advice if it comes from specialists who are senior to them. These reactions were illustrated very clearly in the early days of the nationalization of the coal industry.[2] At the time of nationalization only a dozen or so companies had a staff of specialists and few pits were operated according to the best technical standards. The new management decided to try and raise productivity as quickly as possible and to make the most use it could of the few trained specialists. The best specialists were grouped at head office, with others at the next two levels, division and area. The results were disappointing. Colliery managers were unused to seeking advice, and it proved difficult to persuade them to do so. Visits by technical specialists and suggestions from them tended to be unpopular and to be described as 'interference' and as undermining the manager's authority. The Acton Society Trust, which studied the organization of the National Coal Board at this time, and paid particular attention to line and staff relations, commented:

> An impartial observer cannot regard as satisfactory a situation where, in an industry desperately in need of technical reconstruction, the necessary assistance and advice, provided at great cost, do not prove acceptable to operational management.
>
> Implicit in this whole conception of the role of the specialist, however, is the assumption that management standards can be raised by pressure from above. Whether the specialist is within or without the organization the manager whose standards are low must be induced to consult him. But managers do not, in an industry, always see the defects of their own methods, nor can they, without some instruction, always know what kind of advice the specialist has to offer.
>
> In short, it is only half a solution to make the best technical advice available. It is also necessary to have managers alert enough to make use of this advice, and this is also a problem of education.[3]

The specialist may not only advise, he may also be given authority to issue instructions direct to line management on particular subjects. The authority of the staff department, called 'functional authority' is usually concerned with how things should be done. When specialists are given authority over particular policies or procedures the extent and nature of this authority should be clearly stated so as to try to prevent ambiguity about their power to issue instructions. Yet, as some American writers have remarked:

> it is surprising how many companies, even those otherwise well managed, fail to define the exact nature of functional authority which a manager may have. Study of authority

delegations in a large number of companies shows that adequate clarification in this area is rare.[4]

The danger of functional authority is that it reduces the scope of the manager's job; if many specialists are given such authority it would greatly diminish the manager's responsibility. This happened to such an extent with many foremen's jobs that the foremen claimed they had no responsibility. Some companies tried to remedy these complaints by trying to enlarge the foreman's responsibility and even by giving him his own specialist assistants.

A useful guide in determining whether the staff man needs authority is suggested by Dale. It is: 'What is the worst that can happen if the powers are accorded to the line rather than to the staff?'[5]

The larger the number of specialists who are given functional authority the greater is the danger that their instructions may sometimes conflict. Kaufman, in his study of the forest ranger in the U.S. Forest Service, described the problems that this could create:

> What creates a problem for the field man is the fact that the materials sometimes require mutually exclusive courses of action on his part. The specifications for roads, for example, are generally predicated on engineering premises alone, but roads built to those specifications may conflict with the demands of watershed management or recreation management or timber management specialists. . . . Emphasis on recreation that gratifies recreation officers may disturb fire control officers. What looks like adequate concern for the grazing uses of the national forests may seem like indifference to wildlife management from the perspective of those who specialize in this function. Administrative assistants call for greater attention to office routines and procedures and paperwork, while other functional specia-

lists deplore expenditures of Ranger time in the office
rather than in the woods. Despite the general consensus on
the desirability of multiple-use management, it is not always
clear what this indicates in specific instances.[6]

The geographical separation which is a feature of the
U.S. Forest Service is also found in many large organizations. It adds to the problems that the specialists may
have in appreciating local conditions and to the risk of
conflicting instructions from different departments. The
specialist departments in large organizations may be at
head or divisional offices. This fact can further com-
plicate the relationship between the specialists and the
managers who are in local units. The specialists are liable
to become identified by local management with the 'they',
who do not understand the reality of the operating conditions.

There remains one other type of relationship between
managers and specialists to be discussed, that of the specialist who is outside the organization. This may be easier
than that between line management and the internal specialists. Outside specialists are used for a number of reasons. Small companies, or large companies that need
highly specialist advice, may not have enough work to
justify employing their own specialists, and therefore the
occasional or part-time use of outside specialists is more
economic. They may also use outsiders because the best
specialists may not be attracted to full-time appointments.
The outsider may be able to contribute more because he
has experience of other organizations than he could if
he was employed by only one. Top management may want
to have an outside opinion, so that it is not entirely dependent upon the advice of its own specialists. Top man-

agement, too, may find that it is easier to talk to an outsider as there are none of the reticences on either side that can come from a difference in hierarchical levels. Top management may be loathe to admit ignorance to a subordinate, or to ask questions that may be foolish. They may find it easier to do so to an outsider. Top management may also learn, from the outsider what questions they should be asking their own specialists.

There is another, and quite different, reason for using outside specialists. This is to provide an adequate reason for initiating changes which top management know should be made, but cannot otherwise bring themselves to make. The advice of an outside specialist provides—more particularly if he is highly paid—the pretext for doing so.

There are also dangers in the use of outside specialists. They may not be so responsible in their advice as their careers are less likely to be affected if their advice is shown to be poor. Management, too, tends to be less critical of the recommendations of outside experts. Some top managements are looking for panaceas and will be attracted by those who are peddling the latest one.

SOME SPECIALISTS ARE MORE ACCEPTABLE THAN OTHERS

Discussions about line and staff are sometimes conducted as though all staff functions were the same. Yet a large organization will employ many different types of specialists who will have quite different tasks to perform. McGregor distinguished between the policeman and the professional helper and said that the two were incompatible.[7]

Inspectors and auditors clearly belong to the policeman class and will usually be treated as such. Some staff people, such as the safety officer, may have both functions. Wherever there is a policeman element, this is likely to make it harder for the staff man to be seen as a helper. The tendency will be evasion rather than co-operation.

The distinction between policeman and professional helper, though important, is not the only one that should be made. There are many different kinds of helpers. There are those whose task it is to try to improve the efficiency of management. This is likely to be interpreted by managers as a criticism of the way in which they are working. Hence relations are potentially difficult, and the staff man has to try to persuade line management that he is really seeking to help them.

In research that the author has done into the impact of computers on management in selected companies it was noticeable that relations between line managers and computer specialists were easier when the systems were designed to help in the solution of new problems than they were when the systems were designed to replace existing procedures. In the former the computer specialists were seen as helpful: in the latter they could be seen as interfering in the manager's prerogative.

There are other specialists, such as the personnel staff, who do some part of the manager's job for him. The line manager may resent intrusion into what he thinks is an essential part of his job. The matron, for example, may feel that only she and the principal nurse tutor can interview potential nursing recruits and that a personnel officer could not help. Sometimes there is a danger that, far from resenting interference in his job, the manager may be only too glad to abdicate many aspects of man-management. In one large company the managers had concentrated more and more on the technical aspects of their job, which they found congenial, and left the personnel department to deal with any labour troubles and with all welfare activities. Top management finally decided that this was undesirable abdication from essential aspects of management. In future line management must play a part in labour negotiations and must concern themselves with their employees' welfare; rules were made, for example, about the part that the manager must play after an industrial accident.

The reaction of line managers to the different specialists will be affected, too, by their opinion of the nature of the speciality. The traditional professions are much more easily accepted than the newer specialities. The contribution that their professional training can make is known and accepted. A manager is unlikely to feel any resentment at being given advice by a lawyer, doctor or accountant, since he will not think that such advice is a reflection on his own competence or that it reduces the scope of his job. Lawyers are, perhaps, the most acceptable profession. Newer specialities may receive neither respect nor acceptance. These are now striving to establish the qualifications that will enable them to be accepted as professionals and their efforts seem to be rewarded by a gradual growth of acceptance.

THROUGH THE OTHER'S EYES

The criticisms that managers make of specialists and that specialists make of managers recur so frequently that one can describe a stereotype of the manager, or the specialist, that will be recognizable to members of the other group in most, perhaps in all, organizations.

Managers see the specialist as impractical and out of touch with operational realities; theorists who would be incapable of putting their theories into practice. Even when asked for advice they may be accused of being slow, perfectionist and vague, whereas the manager wants clear advice provided quickly. Hence the old joke about the manager who asked for a one-armed economist, so that he could not say 'On the one hand this, and on the other that'. Managers often complain, too, that the specialists are trying to usurp their authority.

The specialists' picture of the manager is often of a reactionary person who is unwilling to change and who turns down suggestions that would obviously improve the efficiency of his department. They may think of him as touchy and preoccupied with his status. They are likely to see him as inefficient and in great need of their help, a fact which he obdurately refuses to recognize. Even if he does, he is unlikely to know how to ask the right questions.

The two groups are likely to have different views of what they think is important. Specialist groups will probably attach greater importance to high quality than will line management. The latter may merely want something that works, and which can be provided as quickly and cheaply as possible. The specialist will be more interested in the quality of workmanship, both because he gets greater satisfaction from exercising his professional skills and because he may value the opinion of his professional colleagues who will judge him by the quality of what he does. Hence the architect may be more interested in the appearance of his building than in its utility or its cost; the operational researcher may be preoccupied with producing an elegant solution rather than in providing something that will deal with the problem as rapidly as possible. The line manager, if he wishes to attract and retain specialists who are in short supply, such as systems people, will need to understand their viewpoint and to make some allowance for it.

Many professional people are committed to a lifetime's career in their speciality. Their professional goals stress increased knowledge and skill and the solution of more difficult problems. These can clash with the organization's need to have the more humdrum professional work performed, for example, the hernia operations in hospitals and the basic undergraduate teaching in universities.

These differences in viewpoint are often accentuated by other differences. There is frequently an age gap; the specialists tend to be considerably younger, particularly specialists in the newer management techniques. The specialist is more likely to be a graduate. His loyalty may be to his profession, rather than to the organization. In Gouldner's term, he may be a cosmopolitan whereas the line manager is a local.[8] If so he will look for his future career to professional success rather than, as the manager does, to the organization.

The jobs of the two are also different, which affects their attitudes. These differences show themselves in quite simple things like the pattern of the working day. The line manager's day is likely to be much more fragmented than that of the staff specialist. The former will have to deal with a wide variety of subjects and people, often for very short periods. In consequence he will find it hard to plan his day or to find a quiet period for thinking about a problem. The staff man is likely to deal with fewer subjects in a day or a week, and to have less interruptions. He may find it hard to understand why the manager does not take time to analyze a problem.

IMPROVING RELATIONS BETWEEN MANAGERS AND SPECIALISTS

McGregor has a helpful and unusual discussion of how to improve staff-line collaboration.[9] His central consideration is that the appropriate role for staff is that of providing professional help to all levels of management. The relationship should be that of consultant–client. In his view the first prerequisite for improving collaboration is to abandon the requirement that authority and responsibility should be equal, which lays too much emphasis on authority in relationships. The two groups are interdependent; so it is not appropriate to think of line exercising authority over staff. Staff responsibility to all levels of management must be recognized, so staff groups should not be given responsibilities which entail their exercising authority over lower levels of management. McGregor attaches importance to managers practising self-control, so that staff should supply control data to the manager of the unit rather than to his superior.

Two of the organizational locations of the specialist that we have discussed are often used to try to avoid some of the difficulties that arise in relations between line and staff. One is to put the specialist on the managers' staff so that he is personally involved in the department's work, can get to know its problems at first hand, and is likely to be accepted as a colleague instead of being seen as an outsider, one of 'them'. Another advantage is that the manager's authority is not reduced by the presence of specialists outside the department, whose advice he may not feel able to ignore and whose instructions he will have to conform to. Because of these advantages it is worth considering whether specialists should be assigned to a manager's staff, but this is not always practical and may be more costly. The specialist, too, may need to have an additional staff boss who can supervise his professional competence.

The other organizational method of easing relations is to create a specialist department which only provides a service if asked, and sometimes only if paid for. This has the advantage of leaving the initiative, or at least the decision as to use of the specialist's services to the line manager. It has the disadvantage that the managers who may most need the services are the ones who are least likely to use them. Further, when the services have to be paid for there may be accounting problems in the allocation of overheads.

There is yet another organizational method for trying to make specialists acceptable. Its advocates are, not surprisingly, usually the heads of the relevant speciality. It is to put the head of the department high in the hierarchy, preferably reporting to the managing director. This, it is suggested, will ensure that the speciality will be taken seriously and that its advice and services will be used. A senior position for the manager of the specialist department will bring both the advantage of informal contacts and the formal advantages that come from being high up in the hierarchy. If there is a top-management dining-room the specialist head lunching there can develop friendly and informal contacts with the heads of the line departments.

There are two snags to this method of making specialists acceptable. The first is that there are limits to the numbers of specialist departments that can report to the managing director, if his span of control is not to become unwieldy. The other, and more important, snag is that the argument may not be true. McKinsey's second study of computer use in thirty-six large United States and European companies found that an individual's effectiveness depended more on his personal stature and personal skills, than his place in the hierarchy. They discovered, they said, 'no evidence, statistical or otherwise, to suggest that high organizational status assures effective performance on the part of the corporate computer staff'.[10]

A method that is used in some organizations, and most widely by the armed services, to try to reduce differences in attitude between line and staff is rotation between the two types of work, thus preventing the growth of purely specialist personnel. This can only be done where the staff job is not a highly professional one that requires a long training. There is no job rotation for lawyers and doctors. Many of the newer specialities, which require less training, such as personnel, organization and methods, and operational research lend themselves to transfer of personnel across departments. A couple of years in operational research is sometimes used as an initial training for future managers before entering a line department. Some companies have few career people in personnel, but think of this as a function that should be performed for some years by a manager, transferred from a line department, as part of his training for a top appointment. Such rotation helps to avoid the development of too narrowly a specialist outlook. It can also be useful in giving managers some knowledge of the speciality so that they will be in a better position both to use it, and to control its practitioners. However, job rotation between line and staff is no panacea for the problems of relationships between the two. It can help, but with the change of hat a man's viewpoint tends to change too. Misunderstanding and ignorance may be reduced, but there can still be a marked difference in viewpoint.

Project teams, which are set up with a limited life to deal with a particular problem, may be composed of people with both specialist and line-management experience. One by-product of such a team is that members should learn to understand each other's viewpoint. A project team is unlikely to be established for its educational value, and hence cannot be described as one of the methods for improving understanding between specialists and manager. However, individuals might be appointed to such a team as part of their career development.

Finally, there are three tactical guides for the specialist. One is to find out what problem is currently worrying the manager and offer to help. This is true for the personnel man who is trying to convince line management of the need to take management development seriously. He may get nowhere if he talks in general terms, but if there is a sudden problem of finding a suitable replacement he may be able to point out what needs to be done to avoid such problems in future. If top management is worried about its ability to attract good graduates—and such a worry is in itself rather sophisticated—he may be able to offer a useful analysis of why the company is failing to do so and what needs to be done.

The second tactical guide is to start in an area where success is certain, or almost certain. This is the advice offered by some of the computer consultants. Start with something simple, with a sure pay-off, they say. If you start with something that is more ambitious, but which is less certain to succeed, you may have greater success, but if you fail the managers may be disillusioned for a long time. The same tactics are indicated for any new specialist department which is trying to get its services recognized.

The third guide is a negative one. A specialist department that is still struggling to get accepted should try and avoid projects that are likely to raise difficulties for other groups. It may be impossible, or undesirable to do so, but at least the dangers of arousing antagonism should be recognized.

The specialist should always try to involve line management in the project whenever it is feasible to do so. Line management will be more interested if they are involved and more likely to continue to use the service, or to implement the proposals. Moreover the proposals themselves, or the system, may well be more suited to the needs of the department, as the manager will be able to point out some of the practical considerations that may be overlooked by the specialist.

SUMMARY

'Line and Staff', the traditional heading in books on organization, does not cover all the types of problems that arise between managers and specialists. It omits the difficulties that can develop even when the specialist reports solely to the line manager.

Two main distinctions have been made between line and staff. One is based on the department's activities; line departments are those that contribute directly to the organization's objectives. The other, clearer, distinction is based on accountability—line departments are those that are accountable for results.

The problems that arise in relations between managers and specialists vary with the organizational relationship. There are four main types of relationship. One, the specialist is on the manager's staff and has no other organizational link. Two, he is on the manager's staff but also is responsible to a staff boss for his professional competence. Here it is especially important that the organizational relationship should be clarified. Three, he is in a separate department. Four, he is outside the organization and is employed as a consultant. The problems that can exist in these different relationships are discussed.

Some types of specialists are much more acceptable to line managers than others. McGregor distinguishes between the role of the policeman and that of the professional helper: the latter obviously being more acceptable than the former. The respectability of the speciality also affects its acceptability. Advice from old-established professions like medicine or law is not seen as a potential threat to the manager's job as may advice from newer specialities, like operational research.

The outlook of the two groups tends to be very different. They often differ in age, education and in career focus. Their jobs, too, are different and this affects their attitudes.

McGregor suggests a number of ways of improving staff–line collaboration. His central thesis is that the staff should act as a professional helper to all levels of management.

Various organizational means are used to facilitate the relationship. One is to put the specialist on the manager's staff. Another is to have specialist departments which only provide services on request and for a fee. Yet another is to put the head of the specialist department very high in the hierarchy. All these methods have snags. Rotation between staff and line jobs is used in some organizations as a means of reducing differences in attitudes. Project teams composed of people from both line and staff departments can also help to create understanding between them.

Three tactical guides for the specialist are suggested.

.　.　.

1. National Industrial Conference Board, *Corporate Organization Structures* (New York, The Conference Board, 1968) pp. 7–8.

2. Cf. Acton Society Trust, *The Extent of Centralization: A Discussion Based on a Case Study in the Coal Industry,* Part II (The Trust, 1951) p. 27.

3. Ibid., p. 28.

4. Harold Koontz and Cyril O'Donnell, *Principles of Management: An Analysis of Management Functions,* 4th edn (New York, McGraw-Hill; Tokyo, Kogakusha, International Student Edition, 1968) p. 307.

5. Dale, *Organization,* p. 79.

6. Kaufman, *Forest Ranger,* p. 68.

7. McGregor, *The Human Side of Enterprise,* p. 164.

8. Alvis W. Gouldner, 'Cosmopolitans and Locals', *Administrative Science Quarterly,* vol. 2, no. 3 (Dec. 1957) pp. 282–92.

9. Ibid., chap. 12.

10. McKinsey & Co., *Unlocking the Computer's Profit Potential* (New York, 1968) p. 37.

7 Managerial Relations

This is an unusual subject to find in a book on organization. Ignorance was one reason for this omission in the past. Until recently it would have been very difficult to write a descriptive, as distinct from a purely speculative, chapter on managerial relations, as there was so little information about them. Now research has contributed to a better understanding of them, but there is still much that we do not know. Ignorance also led us to underrate the importance of managerial relations to the understanding of how organizations work.

In the past the view of management motivation and behaviour was too simple. The manager tended to be conceived as an economic man, calculating relative profitabilities and acting accordingly. Research has now shown that this conception ignores the other influences upon management behaviour. This chapter will describe what research can tell us about managerial relations. It will discuss how managers deal with each other, how their relations can be affected by the situation of the company, what kind of problems arise in these relations and what can be done to try and reduce them.

A manager is often described as someone who gets things done through other people. We tend to forget that this means that he is dependent upon them. The dependence of the manager on other people is one of the key characteristics of the managerial way of life, a characteristic that increases with the complexity of the job. The manager depends upon his superiors for his advancement, upon his subordinates for the efficiency of his department, and often upon his colleagues at his own level for help in getting his job done. The relationships that he has with his fellow managers are, therefore, vital to the success of his own job and to his future career.

Managerial relations are changing as a result of changes in the environment of the organization and in technology. These changes are making the relations between managers even more important to the effective working of the organization. In the more stable conditions of the past, which still exist for some companies, clearly marked boundaries separated one department from another. The tasks of each department were well known and relations between departments followed well-established channels. Much of the communications between them could be written. Oral communications took place mainly vertically, between superior and subordinate, rather than laterally between members of different departments. In such stable organizations the relations between managers in different departments followed a pattern. The head of each department was the baron of his own domain, subject only to the king, the managing director. Some barons were more important than others, but each knew the boundaries of his own domain and usually respected those of others.

The research of Burns and Stalker has shown how rapid change can affect relations between managers.[1] What has to be done is no longer known; it has to be discovered. This can most easily be achieved by discussion. Managers must spend much more time talking to each other than they need to do in more stable conditions. The boundaries between departments become less clearly defined. The uncertainty that exists in times of change is likely to lead to difficulties in relations between managers and to provide greater opportunities for playing power politics. Managerial relations, therefore, tend to be more difficult and more important when organizations are experiencing rapid change.

TYPES OF RELATIONS

The distinctive feature about relations between managers in different departments is that they depend upon the individual's capacity to get things done through other people without the support of formal authority. This can be true even when he has the approval of top management for a project. One senior manager in a large company who headed a specialist department presented a proposal to a small committee of the Board. They approved. As he left the room one of them said 'Good luck'. It was only later he realized the significance of that remark: even though top management liked his plan, his success would depend upon his ability to enlist the co-operation of other managers.

Sayles has made an illuminating distinction between the different kinds of relations that can exist between managers. He distinguishes seven, which he calls: workflow, trading, service, advisory, auditing, stabilization and innovation.[2] Some of these were discussed in the chapter on The Manager and the Specialist. Here it is appropri-

ate to look at two, the work-flow and the trading relationships. As Sayles says of the first:

> From the manager's point of view, these work-flow re-
> lationships are crucial. How much he can accomplish
> depends upon the condition and timing of the 'work' he re-
> ceives from the one or more preceding stages *and* the de-
> mands made upon him by those other managers for whose
> departments his department is the preceding stage.[3]

This kind of dependence is a strain on the relationships
between the managers of the departments that are con-
nected by a work-flow. There is a tendency to blame
others for delays which make the work of one's own department more difficult. The department that comes earlier in the work-flow can also be a convenient scapegoat
to excuse one's own failings. The character of these relationships depends upon the personalities concerned, their
feelings for each other and their concern for organizational, as distinct from narrowly departmental, objectives.
These relationships can be eased by recognizing their existence and, where feasible, by formalizing them, that is
specifying the responsibilities for each part of the work-
flow and the procedures to be followed. The importance
of these work-flow relations should, therefore, be recognized in the relevant job descriptions, but this is rarely
done except in the most general terms. There is a need,
too, to ensure that managers in a work-flow relationship
keep in touch with each other. This is most necessary
when they are working on something new, otherwise there
is a danger that the work of one section may conflict with
the work of another, in its content or timing.

Another type of relationship that Sayles discusses is
the trading one. He calls this 'the process by which the

terms of some future relationship are established'.[4] One trading relationship can be between service departments and their customers, another, is that between the manager who is responsible for completing a task and the other individuals and groups in the organization whose help he needs to do so. Sayles thinks that although these trading relations within organizations are similar to those between buyers and sellers outside there are some differences. The constraints upon the buyer may be somewhat greater than in the market-place where he can negotiate with other salesmen. There may also be a multi-price system. 'Good friends (or those offering more interesting or desirable projects) may get lower prices than organizational enemies or those requesting less pleasant services.' Sayles bases this latter statement on a study he did of contracting-out versus in-plant maintenance, where great variability in the addition of overhead to various cost estimates was observed.[5]

Sayles sees trading relationships as a crucial aspect of many managers' jobs. He thinks that some managers resent this type of relationship and wish instead for rules to decide who does what, with whom, and on what terms. He suggests that this kind of relationship will become more important as the boundaries of organizations become more fluid. Increasingly, managers will have trading relationships both inside and outside the organization, as a wider variety of work is contracted out.

The price that is paid in a trading relationship between two members of the same organization is not necessarily a monetary one. A service department may sell its services, but often the price is some reciprocal aid. There may be an explicit agreement: 'I will help you, if you will do

so and so.' But it may also be implicit, the recognition of
an obligation which can be drawn on in the future.

Sayles's discussion of trading relationships is concerned
with manufacturing industry, but one can notice similar
relationships in diverse types of organization. Blau and
Scott describe reciprocal consultation in a social service
agency.[6] Where the consultation is only in one direction
the price paid is the acknowledgement that one's colleague
is more expert than oneself. Those who do not want to
acknowledge an inferior status take care not to ask one
person too often for advice. Similar reactions can be found
in universities, where the help that is given to a colleague
either creates a reciprocal obligation, such as to help later
with one of his students, or a difference in informal status.

The type of relationship affects the ways in which managers deal with each other, and the kind of problems that
arise. The differences between managers' jobs also have
an effect, since they influence the viewpoints of their occupants.

DIFFERENCES BETWEEN MANAGERIAL JOBS
The difficulties that often arise in interdepartmental relations are partly due to conflicts between the aims of individual departments. They are also due to differences
in the nature of the jobs and in the personal attributes
that these jobs require. Research is beginning to tell us
more about these differences. An American study looked
at differences between the attributes of managers in four
functions: engineering and research and development;
sales; administration and accounting; and production.[7]
Two hundred and fifty managers in more than a dozen

companies were given intelligence and personality tests and interviews. The main differences between managers in the four functions were found to be in intelligence, education and professional knowledge. There were also some personality differences. Commenting on the effects of one of these differences on interdepartmental relations, the researchers said:

> These findings suggest that, in most companies, the sales group will be the most assertive and the most vocal, and that in promoting this function, its members may tend to take a narrow and somewhat selfish point of view. Such a tendency can be dangerous for the company as a whole and should, therefore, be controlled. Top management should also recognize the dangers of the sales group's tendency to impetuosity. . . . Because of their verbal ability and aggressiveness, sales executives may be able to disclaim responsibility for their errors and project them on other groups in the company.

The author's study of how managers spend their time found that the sample could be divided into five groups distinguished by their different working patterns. The most distinctive group was the one that was mainly composed of production managers. Their working days were more fragmented than those of the other groups of managers. They spent more time with their subordinates than other groups and less time with people outside the department.[8] The working environment of the production manager is very different from that of the sales manager. The sales department is under pressure both from the works and from the customers. The individual salesman may feel personally involved in his relationships with his customers—although this will vary somewhat with the kind of company, as well as with the individual. He will hate to say 'No' to a customer. He will be reluctant to tell him if there is a long delay in delivery. He may try and get special treatment for particular customers, without considering whether it pays the organization to do so or not. In these ways, he is likely to think differently from those in production.

There are just as great contrasts to be found in other types of organizations. The hospital secretary, for example, lives in a different world from that of the matron or the consultant. Such jobs are likely to attract different kinds of people. These differences are strengthened by training. In local government the treasurer comes from a different professional background from the education officer or the medical officer of health; the pattern of his working day and the people he is in contact with are also quite different. These contrasts between the working experience of managers in different occupations and departments intensify the problems of communication between them.

COMMUNICATIONS WITHIN MANAGEMENT

We are generally more conscious of barriers to communications between different levels in the hierarchy than of those between departments. The latter can also be important, especially in times of change when more interdepartmental communications are necessary. At such times it needs to be made easy for people to talk to each other, so that they are not inhibited from asking others for information and advice. Burns and Stalker described well what is wanted:

The operation of an organic system of management hinges on effective communication. This is much more than a matter of providing, through the distribution of paper,

for notification of events and decisions affecting function-
ally related persons and departments. It is also something
more than providing for exchanges of information and
opinion in meetings. What is essential is that nothing should
inhibit individuals from applying to others for information
and advice, or for additional effort. This in turn depends on
the ability to suppress differences of status and of technical
prestige on occasions of working interaction, and on the
absence of barriers to communication founded on functional preserves, privilege, or personal reserve. In one or
two firms, the existence of a way of behaving which facili-
tates this freedom of interaction was their most immediately
obvious characteristic. . . .[9]

In one company Burns and Stalker studied, everybody
was called 'chief'. This helped people to talk to each other
across what otherwise might have been barriers of status.
In another company similar results were achieved by so-
ciability and good manners, perhaps reflecting the managing director's views of the respect due to other people.
Christian names were used widely up and down the status
hierarchy, though the authors thought this was only the
most superficial aspect of this social manner.

The use of christian names is not in itself important. It
may be a national cultural habit to do so, as in the United
States or, not to do so, as in Japan. In Britain practice
varies. The use of christian names may be symptomatic
of the kind of relations that exist in the organization, but
are not likely to be a cause of them. Managers in traditionally strongly hierarchical organizations, such as hospitals, seem to find the suggestion that they might use
christian names disturbing. In hospitals they are rarely
used between colleagues except by doctors, and the idea

that they could be used by the subordinates is thought
to threaten the superior's authority.

THE POWER STRUCTURE

A dominant factor in managerial relations, particularly
at the level of top management, is the existence of a power
structure. This fact is rarely openly acknowledged. Many
managers talk of decision-making as if it was a wholly
rational choice between alternatives, based on the assessment of the profitability of different courses of action in a
business, and on their contribution to furthering the objectives in other organizations. Any observer of the process of decision-making will notice that though arguments
are likely to be couched in rational terms, the relative
weight that is given to different arguments, and the kind
of arguments that are put forward, may well be determined by the policies of the different political factions.
The decision that is reached may depend on the relative
strength of these factions. Few questions are so clear-cut
that there is obviously only one rational decision. Some
decisions, of course, do not affect the power structure but
even then different political factions may develop. For example, the decision as to which make of computer to buy
should not, at first sight, have any effect on the balance
of power between departments, or between individuals.
Yet it can become the source of a political battle between
supporters and opponents of different makes.

The power structure can affect the type of decision that
is reached. It also commonly delays it. The more the decision is likely to affect the balance of power the longer
the delay is likely to be. In government we talk about the

need to reach a politically acceptable decision and the time that it may take to do so. This may mean one that is generally acceptable, or one that is acceptable to the supporters of the party in power. Whichever it is, there are limits to what the government can do. Here the sanction against infringing these limits is that the voters will reject the party that does so. But there are also sanctions in business and other organizations. Senior managers may resign—and in some companies they do—or their enthusiasm and co-operation may decline. Hence most managements will delay reaching a decision that causes strong opposition in the hope that opinions may change, or a more acceptable pretext for the need to take the decision may turn up.

The managing director of a company should be sensitive to the political line-up amongst his senior managers. Otherwise he may make a decision that upsets the power structure too much. The results of one who did so, when confronted with a disagreement between several of his senior managers was like, as one of those present put it, 'the breaking of a very valuable Chinese vase. Everyone stood around horrified and no-one had the resilience to try and pick up the pieces again.'

Power battles are more common at the senior management levels than they are lower down. One explanation is that senior managers who head large departments or divisions have more at stake. Another is that relations are much more personal in the small top-management group. Yet another possible explanation may be that the more politically conscious and ambitious people reach top management. Whatever the reasons, the atmosphere at top-management level, particularly in a large organization, is likely to be different from that lower down. As one junior manager who had to attend senior management meetings said: 'When I tell my contemporaries how senior managers behave, they won't believe me, but then they have not watched these power battles.'

If politics are a fact of organizational life, as the evidence suggests, what is the significance for the reader? The implications for those who want to get promotion have already been described by the author in an earlier book.[10] The implications for would-be innovators, such as operational research workers, are important. It is common for the young specialist and manager, particularly if he is scientifically trained, to believe that logical arguments alone are sufficient to get a proposal accepted. He may be insensitive to the ways in which people react to his proposals and to the importance of trying to persuade them that his ideas are good ones. He may be unaware of the need to discover who are the most powerful people in the organization—not necessarily conveyed by looking at an organization chart—and to make a special effort to convince them of the value of his proposals, or at least to try and ensure that he does not antagonize them.

The implications of the prevalence of power politics are important for top management too. The managing director, and other top managers, create conditions that encourage or discourage power politics. When there are issues that affect the interests of powerful individuals or groups, the discussion should be aimed at trying to resolve the problem rather than at creating a win or lose situation. Here the example set by top management and especially by the managing director, or by the chairman of a committee discussing the issue, can help to set the tone of the discussion.

Top management can also set the climate within which competition for promotion will be conducted. The steeper the organizational pyramid, the fiercer the competition is likely to be for the small number of top jobs. The greater the emphasis on the desirability of promotion, and the less satisfying the middle-level jobs, the more competition there is also likely to be. Organizations vary widely in the ways in which this competition is conducted. Public organizations seek to depersonalize promotion and to make it as objective as possible. Companies normally have a much less formalized, more secretive approach to deciding who shall be promoted. In both, but more especially in companies, promotion is likely to be a subject for power politics. The more senior the appointment, the more of it there is likely to be. This is a fact that those responsible for making the appointment should recognize, and try to avoid exacerbating.

The example set by the managing director is vital to the climate of the organization and to the ways in which politics are conducted. Burns and Stalker call this a code of conduct and say that: 'The code is fixed—consciously or unconsciously, deliberately or by default—by the managing director. It is his most important contribution to the welfare of the organization.'[11]

CREATING LOYALTY TO ORGANIZATIONAL GOALS

One of the reasons for power politics is that individuals and departments identify with their own goals rather than with those of the organization as a whole. Departments are likely to develop their own aims, which may conflict with each other as well as with the company's aim of maximizing profitability. A prime problem, therefore, is how to get managers to subordinate their individual and local aims to the aims of the organization as a whole. The larger the organization the greater the problem is likely to be.

Katz describes how this organizational loyalty was achieved amongst the top management of one company.[12] He studied the behaviour of the president (managing director) and the six senior executives of a medium-sized American company in a consumer-goods industry. Each of the senior executives either headed a function, such as production or sales, or a product division. Katz said that collaboration amongst this top-management group was facilitated by the following factors:

1. *A well-defined social structure* which came from the long experience that six of the seven executives had in working together in their present positions. Their relative statuses and roles had become established, so had their codes of behaviour.

2. *Shared values.* Katz gives a number of examples, among them the fact that five of the executives were primarily sales-oriented.

3. *Acknowledgement of technical 'expertise',* each of the seven was recognized as the technical expert on particular problems.

4. *Free interchange* encouraged by little stress on titles or job descriptions, consultations with people at any level who had relevant expertise, and a physical layout with few partitions or walls.

5. *Identification with the company* because each of the top executives thought that his reputation depended upon the success of the company as a whole.

6. *Penalties for deviant behaviour* by, for example, withdrawing support from anyone who did not observe the norms described above, such as free interchange.

7. *Organizational structure built around individuals.* 'Each man performed those duties in which he was perceived as having greater ability than anyone else in the organization, in which he had interest, and in which he felt most comfortable. Advancement depended largely on ability to understand and utilize the system of informal interchange, and to establish one's own acknowledged area of competence.'

8. *A team with all necessary skills.* 'In the top management group, there existed adequate technical skill to cope with the company's most important recurring problems, sufficient human relations skill to maintain a high degree of interpersonal respect, and a well-defined 'conceptual skill' (in the president) for visualizing the relationships of the various aspects to one another.'

The role of the president as the prime co-ordinator was well-established, but it led to domination by the president and dependency on the part of his senior executives.

Other companies may use other methods as there is no single set of answers to the problem of how to create a corporate loyalty. However, there are a number of different ways of encouraging managers to identify with the organization's goals. Shared beliefs—that is, a common management philosophy—are important. This is a consideration that is sometimes taken into account by managements when discussing a possible merger. It can be disruptive to attempt to merge with a company whose managers have a different philosophy about, for example, the way to treat employees. Participation in the formulation of objectives is another, and complementary, way of trying to achieve identification with common objectives.

Managers in different departments and in different occupations will, as we have seen, have dissimilar job experiences and may have different personality characteristics. To offset these differences there needs to be opportunities for shared experiences and for the development of common beliefs. In a small organization departmental managers will be in close contact with each other but in large organizations they can be quite isolated. Common experience can be provided by interdepartmental job transfers, by internal training courses, and by other opportunities for managers to get together. Managers' dining-rooms are one useful means of doing this, and so are interdepartmental meetings, unless they become power battle-grounds. The occasional residential conference for managers can be a good way of identifying goals and encouraging a sense of participation in them.

Corporate loyalty has its dangers as well as its advantages.[13] Managers may identify too much with the organization so that they lose the capacity for looking critically at it. They may produce too few new ideas themselves and be unreceptive to new ideas from outside. This can lead to stagnation. It is a danger that large organizations, especially those which aim to do all their recruiting direct from schools and universities, need to guard against.

SUMMARY

The nature of the relations that exist between managers is an important factor in determining how the organization works. The chapter describes what research can tell us about these relations. Managers are dependent upon other managers for the success of their work, not only dependent upon their boss and their subordinates but also upon their colleagues at the same level. The importance of relations between colleagues increases in times of change, when much more lateral communication is necessary.

There are many different types of relations between managers. Sayles describes seven. Two are discussed in this chapter: the work-flow and trading relations. Both can be crucial for the success of a manager's own work.

Relations between managers are made more complicated by the fact that they often work in very different types of jobs. These jobs tend to attract different personalities and these differences are accentuated by training and experience.

Effective relations between managers depend upon good communications. This is most important in times of change when it is essential that people should be able to talk freely to each other without feeling inhibited in asking for information and advice.

Power politics are a characteristic of organizational life. This fact can affect the nature of decisions that are made and the time it takes to make them. A sensitivity to the power politics of an organization can be important for the man who wants promotion, for the would-be innovator and for top management. The latter can seek to shift the emphasis in a discussion from win-or-lose to a problem-solving approach. The managing director sets the code of conduct within which managerial relations take place.

All organizations need to try and create a corporate loyalty so that managers identify with the organization's goals, instead of too narrowly with their individual or departmental goals. This can be helped by the provision of common experiences and by the development of shared beliefs. But it should not be forgotten that corporate loyalty can also have its dangers.

. . .

1. T. Burns and G. M. Stalker, *The Management of Innovation,* (London, Tavistock, 1967).

2. Leonard R. Sayles, *Managerial Behavior: Administration in Complex Organizations* (New York, McGraw-Hill, 1964) pp. 49–51.

3. Ibid., p. 68.

4. Ibid., p. 60.

5. Ibid., p. 62.

6. Peter M. Blau and Richard W. Scott, *Formal Organizations: A Comparative Approach* (London, Routledge & Kegan Paul, 1963; paperback 1966) pp. 128–39.

7. L. Hutter, S. Levy, E. Rosen and M. Stopol, 'Further Light on the Executive Personality', *Personnel,* vol. 36, no. 2 (Mar–Apr 1959) pp. 42–50. Reprinted in S. G. Huneryager and I. L. Heckman, *Human Relations in Management,* 2nd edn (South Western, 1967) pp. 153–62.

8. Stewart, *Managers and their Jobs,* chap. 6.

9. Burns and Stalker, *The Management of Innovation,* p. 252.

10. Roy Lewis and Rosemary Stewart, *The Boss: The Life and Times of the British Business Man* (London, Phoenix House, rev. edn, 1960; Aldine paperback) chap. IV.

11. Burns and Stalker, *The Management of Innovation,* p. 252.

12. Extracts from unpublished doctoral dissertation, Harvard

Business School, 1956; Robert L. Katz, 'Executive Teamwork: Top Management Co-ordination in a Medium-Sized Company', in Paul R. Lawrence, *Organizational Behavior and Administration: Cases, Concepts, and Research Findings* (Homewood, Illinois, Richard D. Irwin and Dorsey Press, rev. edn, 1965) pp. 602–4.

13. Highlighted by William H. Whyte in *The Organization Man* (London, Cape, 1957).

8 How Much Decentralization?

Two of the most important decisions to be made in any organization are: 'How decentralized should the organization be?' and 'What decisions should be delegated?'[1] These are the questions discussed in this chapter. The first question is about general policy, the second asks about the way in which it should be implemented.

The head of a very small business does not have to decide what decisions he should delegate, since he can make them all himself. He may continue to try and do so as his business grows, but its future success will depend, in part, both on his willingness to delegate and on his ability to decide correctly what decisions he should delegate and which ones he should take himself.

The boss who does not delegate—that is, who does not give his subordinates authority to act—will find that even though he appoints extra staff to ease his load they are always coming to him for decisions. He will have no opportunity to think, at least while he is at work, about the main problems of his business, as he will always be being asked about details. He may become like the managing director of a medium-sized family firm who had to see his visitors in the waiting-room because his office was full of papers awaiting his attention and besieged by staff wanting decisions.

WHAT IS DECENTRALIZATION?

All organizations can be pictured as somewhere on a continuum with centralization at one end, and decentralization at another. At no point can one draw a line and say that those on one side are centralized and those on the other are not. One can only talk about organizations as being more or less centralized or decentralized. Even then there are difficulties. How do you compare the extent of centralization in different organizations? A number of research workers have suggested indices for doing so. The most straightforward is that used in an American Management Association's questionnaire survey in the mid-1960s, which asked questions like: who makes the final decisions for the company as a whole, or for a particular division of it, on such matters as pricing policy, salaries over a certain level and the creation of new departments? Are there definite limits set on expenditure, if so, what amount of money requires the approval of the Board?[2]

Pugh and his colleagues have devoted a lot of research effort to developing indices for comparing different types of organizations. One of their indices is of centralization, which resembles the corresponding A.M.A. index, except that they use a more refined way of comparing the levels at which decisions are taken. They developed a standard list of thirty-seven recurrent decisions and asked: 'Who is the last person whose assent must be obtained before legitimate action is taken even if others have subsequently to confirm the decision?' Organizations were scored from 0 to 5 for each decision, according to the level at which the decision was taken. The total score on the thirty-seven items was the measure of the amount of centralization.[3]

Truman has summarized a number of indices of decentralization—they could equally well be used as indices of the amount of centralization—in public authorities.[4] He gives these as:

1. the extent to which 'local co-ordinators' supervise field specialists;
2. 'the frequency with which field offices refer matters to headquarters for decision';
3. 'the number and specificity of general regulations or special directions under which the field agents work';
4. 'the provision for appeal from the decision of field agents';
5. the number of decisions on individual cases made by field men, and the variety of duties performed by them.

These authors have used factual measures to assess the amount of centralization or decentralization. Yet this approach has its limitations, as Kaufman points out:

If experimentation discloses that field behaviour can be controlled as effectively by inculcating the fact and value premises of central headquarters upon the minds of field men *without* extensive use of close supervisory and enforcement procedures, as is possible *with* these devices, then an organization which gives every indication of decentralization by all the usual indices may in fact be as fully governed from the centre as one without these visible paraphernalia of central direction. . . . The usual criteria stress external forms and tend to neglect actual behaviour.[5]

HOW MUCH DECENTRALIZATION?

There is no easy answer to the question 'How much decentralization should there be?' The answer may well vary both with the type of organization and with the stage in its development. The size of the organization is obviously important: the larger it is the stronger the arguments for decentralization, because of the problems of effectively controlling a large organization from the centre, and at the same time giving junior and middle managers some scope for initiative. There are other factors that must be considered too. One of these is the diversity of activities and the extent to which top management can adequately understand them. It is easier to centralize effectively a large company which is engaged in one main activity, such as steel-making, than a company which is engaged in a variety of dissimilar activities. The rate of change may also limit the amount of centralization that is possible; where operating conditions are changing rapidly more may have to be left to the judgement of the man on the spot. Moreover, rapidly changing technology may enforce delegation of some decisions because it is likely to be the junior staff who are most technically up to date and who understand the latest developments.

The amount of decentralization that top management thinks is desirable will depend on how far it wants common policies. If it favours common policies in the main areas of the business it can still decentralize provided that there are well-established procedures and a common management outlook, to give top management some assurance that the organization will continue to be managed in a consistent way. It is more difficult to achieve this combination of objectives in a newly created organization that is composed of many undertakings which were previously separate. Examples of this are the British nationalized coal and electricity industries, which were formed by bringing together hundreds of separate undertakings. Both these industries followed a more centralized policy for the first few years after nationalization than they did later, because of the need to try and get some uniformity in policies and procedures. Public organizations that are expected to have consistent policies in the treatment of their clients or employees must be more centralized than most organizations which are not under such an obligation.

The calibre of staff at all levels will also affect the amount of decentralization that is possible. Decentralization presupposes staff who are competent to take decisions, both in terms of their ability and their knowledge. Developing countries are usually short of skilled workers and experienced clerical and managerial staff, so that there may be few suitable people to delegate to. Companies opening up subsidiaries in such countries may find that they have to rethink what kind of decisions should be taken at different levels.

These are the factors that affect how much decentralization is practicable or desirable, but the answer that top management gives to the question 'How much decentralization?' will also depend upon its philosophy. Does top management believe that their juniors must learn by being given the freedom to make mistakes? Does it think that people work harder if they are given plenty of scope for initiative, or does it believe that people tend to be lazy and need to be directed and controlled to ensure that they do what is wanted? Does top management believe that it necessarily knows best, that there is no substitute for the years of experience that it has had? The kind of answers that management gives to such questions will determine whether it favours a policy of centralization or one of decentralization.

BALANCING ADVANTAGES AND DISADVANTAGES

Unfortunately for the organization planner—and that term should include, at least to some extent, every manager—both centralization and decentralization have advantages and disadvantages. The aim should, therefore, be to try and find out what is the most appropriate balance between the two extremes for a particular organization in the circumstances that operate at that time. The advantages of centralization are the disadvantages of decentralization and vice versa, so that we need only consider the advantages and disadvantages of one of them. Let us look at decentralization.

Advantages of decentralization

1. It encourages initiative.

2. It makes junior and middle management jobs more interesting.

3. (1) and (2) make it easier to recruit good managers and retain them.

4. It is easier to judge managers' performances if they are made responsible for a decentralized unit of the organization.

5. Decisions are more likely to be taken by those who will have to live with their results.

6. Decisions made closer to the actual situations are likely to be more realistic.

7. Decisions are likely to be made more quickly.

Disadvantages of decentralization

1. It is harder for top management to exercise control over what people are doing, or even to know what decisions they are taking.

2. There is a danger that the perspective of managers of decentralized units may be too limited. They may think too much in terms of local advantage and not enough about the good of the organization as a whole.

3. Administrative costs are likely to be greater because decentralized units will probably have their own specialists.

Management's view as to what is the most suitable balance between centralization and decentralization often changes over a period of time. There is unlikely to be a stable equilibrium between the advantages and disadvantages of the chosen policy. A policy of greater decentralization, for example, is likely to have continuing and, perhaps, snowballing effects. Top management may feel that the managers lower down have taken too much initiative and have got too much out of their control. Alternatively, if top management has been following a policy of centralization of many decisions, it may find that it is losing some of its brighter young men, or that managers lower down are not taking initiative even when top management expects them to.

There are pessimists who believe that you are more likely to get the advantages of centralization or decentralization in the early stages of a change to one or the other, and that the disadvantages will gradually become more evident, so that another change becomes desirable. This may explain why large organizations have often changed their policy several times and in different directions. As one top manager put it: 'You begin to think you ought to change because you become more conscious of the failings of your present policy and persuade yourself that a change must surely be an improvement.'

CRITERIA FOR DELEGATION

We have talked about decentralization in general as a policy that management may choose to adopt. Once such a policy decision is made there comes the difficult problem of deciding what should be delegated and to whom, or, in a large organization, to what level in the hierarchy. One simple answer is that important decisions should be taken at the top, moderately important decisions in the middle and minor decisions near the bottom of the hierarchy. This implies, of course, that management has assessed the relative importance of different decisions.

Top management needs to decide what decisions matter most to the success of the organization. The answer will vary from industry to industry. In pharmaceuticals or computer manufacturing, research and development decisions are the most vital to the success of the company. In many consumer-goods industries marketing decisions are the most important. In the oil industry assessment of international political risks is a major consideration for top management. Efficient production and good marketing policies are of little avail if supplies of oil are cut off and no adequate alternatives developed. In all organizations a supply of good managers will be important for its future success. In the British Civil Service one of the guides to the importance of a decision is whether it is in a politically sensitive area, where a decision may lead to a question in the House of Commons.

The relative importance of a decision, judged by its effect on the organization's objectives, is one guide to who should take the decision. There are a number of other criteria, but they are less clear-cut. The most important are:

What information is necessary to take the decision? Who has this information?

What knowledge is necessary to take the decision? Who has this knowledge?

How quickly, accurately and cheaply can the information be transferred to those with the necessary knowledge?

What are the likely consequences of taking a wrong decision? How important is it that the best decision should be taken?

How urgent is the decision? What are the consequences of a delay in taking it?

The relative importance of these different guides will depend both upon the characteristics of the organization and upon management's policy. In selling and in buying the ability to take a rapid decision may sometimes make the difference between a deal and no deal. In companies where this is so, decisions may have to be delegated to the man on the spot, subject perhaps to a telephone query to his boss. Speed may be vital in saving the life of an injured person so that there may not be time to wait for a more knowledgeable person to give his or her opinion. Yet even here the importance attached to speed will depend upon the environment. In the United States doctors are reluctant to stop to attend to people injured in motor accidents because of the danger that the patient or his relatives may sue the doctor for inadequate treatment.

Banks differ in the importance they attach to a speedy decision when a customer asks for a loan. The management of a bank which has a policy of letting customers know quickly whether they can have a loan is more likely to delegate this authority than a bank where the management has different priorities.

Some decisions need two kinds of knowledge: that which comes from having the feel of the local situation and that which comes from knowing where the local situation fits into the wider picture. The man on the spot may understand the local situation better than a more experienced, more highly trained man who is in a distant office, but the latter is in a better position to judge the possible effect of a local decision on other parts of the organization. Hence the need to decide what decisions need this wider perspective, which may have nothing to do with ability but only reflect the type of job and the location. This was strikingly shown by one manager who was standing in for his chief at a divisional office. While he was there he disallowed some of the requests that he had made in his normal job. Asked why he had done so, he replied that 'It looks different from here'. The works manager is likely to understand John Jones, the shop steward, better than the industrial relations specialist at head office, but the latter is more likely to be able to assess the possible repercussions of a decision in one plant on shop stewards in other parts of the company.

We have talked as though management always made a conscious choice about where decisions should be taken. However, decisions are not always the result of a deliberate choice. They can emerge without anybody being certain who has taken the decision, when it was taken, or even aware that a decision was made.

Management should consider what kind of decisions should be taken at different levels in the organization, but it should also remember that what is decided in theory may well be different from what happens in practice. On the one hand, people may be frightened to accept responsibility for decisions and so push them back up the line. On the other hand, some individuals may take decisions that should have been referred to their boss. Management needs to check from time to time to see where decisions are actually being taken, or whether they are being taken at all. One advantage that some companies have obtained from systems analysis is a knowledge of where some decisions are actually made. This can be a shock, as in one large company where it emerged that vital decisions were being taken by a clerk and were not being reviewed.

TRENDS: MORE DECENTRALIZATION?

The number of large organizations has been increasing, and so has their size. This has led to more interest in decentralization. The trend in the United States in the 1950s was towards greater decentralization, achieved mainly by dividing companies into divisions on a product or geographical basis. In the mid-1960s, according to Dale's report of a survey by the American Management Association, some companies were moving back to greater centralization.[6] Of the hundred companies employing more than 5000 people which answered the survey questionnaire, 54 said that they were moving towards more decentralization of decisions, but 36 said they were moving towards more centralization. Of the 58 medium-sized companies employing between 500 and 5000 people which replied, 32 said that they were moving towards decentralization and 26 said that the trend was towards centralization. A few gave mixed answers indicating decentralization of some activities and centralization of others. Unfortunately there is no information available on these trends in the United Kingdom.

There are those who argue that managements have only decentralized because they had to, because they could not cope with the information required for centralized decision-making. If it became easier for them to cope, then they would want to have more centralization. This is the argument of writers who have predicted that computers would lead to greater centralization, as they can provide top management with more and better information.[7] So far there is no clear evidence that this is happening. The computer may reduce the number of decisions that *must* be decentralized because the information can now be made quickly available for senior management. It may not affect the judgement of what decisions *should* be decentralized. Top management's decision on 'should' will be made in part from its philosophy and in part from its judgement of what are the key areas of the business to which it ought to be attending.

SUMMARY
The chapter discussed two of the most important de-

cisions to be made in any organization: 'How decentralized should the organization be?' and 'What decisions should be delegated?'

There is no clear dividing-line between centralization and decentralization. One can only talk about organizations as being more or less centralized or decentralized. The simplest way of comparing the relative centralization of different organizations is by asking who makes the final decisions on specific subjects, and what sum of money requires Board sanction. Research workers have suggested other measures. Yet these formal measures do not tell us how much central control is exercised by means of indoctrination in company values.

The amount of decentralization that a management will adopt will depend on a variety of factors. Management philosophy will be important. Top managers may believe in the virtues of decentralization or in the merits of centralization. A very large organization will find it harder to work a policy of centralization successfully. Well-established procedures and a common management outlook will make it easier to decentralize without losing control. The diversity of the organization's activities, the rate of change affecting it and the calibre of its staff are all relevant to deciding how much decentralization there should be.

The advantages and disadvantages of centralization or decentralization are described. In very general terms centralization improves control, decentralization makes for flexibility and encourages the use of initiative.

Top management has to decide what to delegate and to whom. It should concentrate on the decisions that are most vital for the organization. A number of criteria for deciding where decisions should be taken are described. Sometimes a knowledge of the local situation may be vital, for other decisions a view of the wider implications for the organization as a whole will be needed. Management should consider where decisions ought to be taken, but it should remember that what happens in practice may be very different from what it thinks or plans, so that it can be salutary to check on where and how decisions are actually being made.

A study in the United States in the 1960s showed that although the majority of companies replying said that they were moving to greater decentralization, a third of the large companies and nearly half of the medium-sized ones said that the trend was to centralization.

. . .

1. In some large companies decentralization may mean the establishment of subsidiary companies with responsibility for their own profit and loss. Delegation then takes place within the subsidiary companies and only the profit-and-loss responsibility may be delegated by the parent company.

2. Dale, *Organization,* chap. 6.

3. D. S. Pugh, D. J. Hickson, C. R. Hinings and C. Turner, 'Dimensions of Organization Structure', *Administrative Science Quarterly,* vol. 13, no. 1 (June 1968) pp. 65–105.

4. D. B. Truman, *Administrative Decentralization* (Chicago, University of Chicago Press, 1940) pp. 56–9. Quoted in Kaufman, *Forest Ranger,* p. 231.

5. Kaufman, *Forest Ranger,* pp. 230–1.

6. Dale, *Organization,* pp. 118–19.

7. Cf. Harold J. Leavitt and Thomas Whisler, 'Management in the 1980s', *Harvard Business Review* (Nov–Dec 1958) pp. 41–8.

9 Order versus Flexibility

We saw in the last chapter that the problem is to strike the right balance between centralization and decentralization, rather than to regard these as alternatives. The same is true for another important aspect of organizations, the degree of formalization. This means the establishment, usually in writing, of definite policies and procedures. Formalization is also characterized by a reliance on written rather than oral means of communication. As the title of this chapter suggests, the choice that has to be made is between the relative advantages of order and flexibility. These two can be seen as the opposite ends of the scale of formalization—the more formalization, the more order and the less flexibility. No organization can successfully set order as its overriding aim, nor can any put flexibility as its prime concern. All organizations need elements of both, and the problem is to decide what is the appropriate balance between them. The aim of this chapter is to help the manager to make this decision so that he can tell when it is desirable to formalize and when formalization may have gone too far.

A particular organization, especially if it is a large one, may be much more formalized in some parts than in others. This may be the result of deliberate design to meet obviously different conditions or it may be an unplanned reaction to the problems of dealing with different circumstances. Within the armed services, for example, long-

established units may be more formalized and more hierarchical than those concerned with newer activities. In
the air force, helicopters are said to be less formalized,
but surprisingly, at least to an outsider, this is not said to
be true of helicopters in the navy. Insiders could probably
explain the difference.

Formalization starts with the establishment of policy
decisions—'establishment' is in itself a word that suggests
formality, and so does 'procedure'. The successful head
of a growing business knows that one way of reducing
the frequency with which his staff come to him for decisions is to establish policies that tell them what to do, or
within what limits they can make a decision. Some kind
of sales policy, for example, soon becomes necessary.
Who should get discounts? Is it a customer who buys a
certain quantity? One who pays cash? One whom one
wants to tempt away from a competitor? One of the employees or a friend of the boss? And so on. The managing director can decide each case as it comes up, or he
can leave it, intentionally or by default, to the discretion
of his staff, or he can formulate a policy to tell them which
categories of people are to get discounts. There will be
cases that the policy does not cover, and so the managing
director must also give his sales manager some guidance
as to when he should use his own discretion and when
he should refer back.

In what areas is it sensible for the chief to make policy
decisions? There must be sufficient continuity and similar-
ity in the types of decisions to be taken that a policy can
cover most of them. For example, discounts are given to
customers buying more than a certain quantity and to
those paying cash. The terms for unusually large orders

may need to be decided individually. The extent to which it is desirable for the managing director to establish policies will depend, in part, on how much change there is. If the market is very competitive and rapidly changing, sales policies will need to be reviewed frequently and much more discretion may have to be given to the man on the spot. It will, therefore, be less advantageous to formalize sales policies. For a product with a relatively stable market, like refined sugar, sales policies will only need to be reviewed infrequently when something happens to disturb the market. For products like washing-machines, that have a more fluctuating market, sales policies will need to be reviewed more often.

Top management can formulate policies, but this does not necessarily mean that they are carried out. It is important to remember that organizations are usually less formalized in practice than a description of the formal organization would suggest. Management at head offices may describe company policy in considerable detail, to a visiting research worker, but discussions with management in the field often shows that this bears little or no resemblance to what happens in practice. What operating managers are doing is likely to be a lot less tidy than the scheme devised in the relative peace of a head office, whether it is the procedure to be followed in filling a vacant post, or the policy to be adopted in deciding on the selling price. One large company designed a sophisticated method for deciding on what quantities of each product the sales department should aim to sell and at what prices. A manager from head office, on a field trip, found out almost by chance that what the salesmen actually did was to give whatever discount they thought necessary to get the business. This action upset the validity of the careful calculations made at head office on the relative profitabilities of different products.

ADVANTAGES OF FORMALIZATION

1. *Clarity of policy*

The value of a clear statement of policy as a way of giving subordinates more freedom of action is often not understood. Subordinates who are given no policies to guide their actions may appear to have great freedom, but they may instead feel inhibited by the knowledge that their boss will hold them responsible for whatever they do, although they are not sure what it is he wants. One senior civil servant described, at a seminar, how he felt freer to take decisions when he knew the Minister's mind. With a Minister whose wishes were less clear, he felt that he had to check back more frequently.

Wilfred Brown, former chairman of Glacier Metal, has argued strongly in favour of the liberating effects of formulating policy:

> Thus, I personally believe that the more formalization that exists, the more clearly we will know the bounds of discretion which we are authorized to use, *and will be held responsible for,* and [that] prescribed policies make clear to people the area in which they have freedom to act. Without a clearly defined area of freedom there is no freedom. This, in fact, is a very old story reaching down through the history of mankind: *there is no real freedom without laws.*[1]

The clear formulation of policy has a further advantage: it stimulates management thinking. If one is going to formulate a policy one has to think about one's objectives and about the best way to achieve them. The effort of doing so can help management to think more critically about what it is doing. It is all too easy to think only vaguely, if at all, about what the policies should be.

2. *Security or certainty*

Closely allied to clarity of policy is the advantage that comes from knowing what to expect. Clearly stated policies, formal procedures and rules can tell both employees and clients not only what they can and cannot do, but also what they will receive. A man knows when he will have to retire and how much pension he will get. The citizen knows what is the rate of taxation: the abolition of arbitrary taxation was one of the early demands of Parliamentarians. The customer knows how much discount he will get if he pays cash.

Formalization also provides another type of security, that which comes from knowing what to do. This is most valuable in conditions of stress. It provides a framework of the known which helps the individual to cope with a frightening situation. This is one reason why the armed services and hospitals are more formalized than most businesses. It is also easier to fit in when one is moved in a highly formalized organization, than it is in an organization where one knows less what to expect.

Temperamentally, of course, people vary in the value that they attach to security and certainty. A few people thrive best in a freewheeling atmosphere, but most people are happiest where there is some structure to tell them what they should do, while some feel unhappy unless there is a clearly defined structure.

3. *Speed and efficiency*

Those who equate formalization with red tape will think it odd, even laughable, to say that it can make for speed and efficiency. Yet formal procedures can economize both on the time that must be spent considering what to do and the time it takes to do it. Once the best method of doing something has been worked out, it can be established as a formal procedure. All that is needed is an occasional review to check that it still is the best method. People get used to doing things in the prescribed way and can become very efficient at doing so. Good formal procedures can make for speed and efficiency, but bad ones can be cumbersome and time-consuming, as we all know.

4. *Control*

The establishment of formal procedures for carrying out different actions helps to ensure predictability of performance and thus to improve control. In large organizations it is common to establish procedures for such actions as filling vacancies, requisitioning stores and paying travelling expenses, but the extent to which these are formalized varies greatly. In one organization there will be the most detailed procedures laid down for every step in the process of filling a vacant job. In another, just as large, there will be no common procedures; each establishment develops its own, which may be comparatively informal.

The degree of formalization depends in part, on the importance that is attached to control. In the public service this is usually greater than in private business, because of the requirement of public accountability. Government departments have to have more control, hence more formalized procedures, than do the nationalized industries. The former are subject to questions in Parliament for matters of day-to-day management, but only on broader policy issues. The Post Office when it was a government department had questions in the House about individual sub-post offices. When it became a public corporation such detailed questions were no longer admissible.

5. *Equity*

Formalization of personnel policies and of methods of dealing with clients can ensure that people get the same treatment. Employees who have worked for a year get so many weeks' sick pay. Men retire at 65, women at 60, and so on. Such decisions are no longer left to the discretion of the man's boss. The main advantage of such formalization is that it ensures similar treatment for all those who fit the rules. What will happen is predictable. Men know when they will retire. The nurse knows what is to be done with a deceased patient's belongings. This certainty protects the person who has to administer the rule from the pressures of special pleading. It also protects the individual from the personal biases of officials and superiors.

DISADVANTAGES OF FORMALIZATION

We said at the beginning, that order and flexibility can be seen as opposite ends of a line drawn to represent different degrees of formalization. The advantages of formalization are predominantly those associated with order. The disadvantages are mainly, but not solely, those of inflexibility.

1. *Discourages initiative*

This is the reverse of the coin of predictability of performance. The aim of such predictability is to discourage initiative. This is desirable when you are in a position to predict what performance you want, but often this will not be possible. Circumstances may vary too much or change too frequently for it to be sensible to establish a formal procedure. Such procedures are designed to deal with unchanging circumstances, or with a number of alternatives that can be specified in advance. They can be more of a handicap than a help when people have to deal with unforeseen situations.

The danger of discouraging initiative is that people with only moderate initiative may lose even that if they have never had occasion to exercise it at work. Those more strongly endowed will probably leave the organization because they find it too restricting.

It should not be assumed that all formalization discourages initiative. We saw in the discussion of advantages that the formulation of policy can provide the framework within which staff know that they can exercise initiative; where this is so they may feel freer to do so.

2. *Promotes deception*

The cynic could maintain that all formalization actively encourages initiative rather than the reverse. Granick, in his study of Russian managers, showed how they circumvented official rules.[2] Dalton, in his description of an American company, showed the initiative that managers in a local plant displayed in providing the form but not the substance of head office requirements.[3] Human beings become very adept at finding ways round rules and procedures if they think that it is in their interest to do so. The deviser of rules and procedures needs to remember this fact and try not to set rules that are an incentive to deception—tax officials need no such warning!

3. *Handicaps adaptation to change*

People who rely on following formal procedures tend to get set in their ways. If circumstances change they may be slow to realize it and slow to adapt. Those who are used to doing things one way often resent having to change to another. People who are used to varying conditions are more likely to adjust easily to changes than those who are used to a stable environment.

4. *Insensitivity*

Equity was described as one of the advantages of formalization. Insensitivity is the other side of the picture, since it is difficult to devise rules that take account of all types of hard cases. To guard against this danger some discretion is allowed, for example, to local officers in the rules governing supplementary social security payments.

Retirement policies are a good example of some of the advantages and disadvantages of formalization. Retirement is something that can easily be formalized as a person's age is then an automatic criterion for when he should retire. One of the merits of formalization, as we saw, is certainty: people know what to expect. It is also an easier policy to administer than one that leaves discretion to the individual. This ease and certainty, though, is achieved at the expense of flexibility. A man's age is, as studies of ageing have shown, a very crude guide to the decline in a person's usefulness. People age at different rates so that one man of 65 may be physically and mentally younger than another at 60. Even amongst those who age at the same rate some contribute much more than others. Many organizations try to have retirement policies that make provision for early retirement, which may be voluntary or compulsory. They may also, as in the Civil Service, have a provision that although everyone retires at a fixed age, some can be invited to stay on for a further period. Such retirement policies aim to secure some flexibility so that a few individuals may retire earlier or later, while retaining most of the advantages of certainty.

Managers need to weigh the advantages and the disadvantages of formalization. Usually, it is not a simple question of deciding for or against rules or procedures, but rather of deciding how general or how specific and detailed they should be. Formalization is most useful in stable conditions. It can be a handicap in rapidly changing conditions and where initiative from the man on the spot is essential.

Management in a very formalized organization must take steps to try and protect itself from the dangers of ossification. Kaufman describes how the U.S. Forest Service, which is highly formalized, seeks to do this.

The Forest Service, despite its success in injecting its own outlook into its men, has avoided many of the hazards of success; it has preserved a good deal of its own flexibility. Alert to the dangers, the leaders frequently engage outside consultants to check their methods and procedures, grant leaves for their members to get additional university training . . . encourage personnel to become active in professional associations and societies, open their doors to social science researchers, circulate current literature throughout the agency, and otherwise invite and seek out developments and innovations in all fields. . . .

. . . the elaboration of staff units represents a decision to promote studies and reflection by men free of line responsibilities and duties, men who are expected to generate new practices, and to prod line administrators into applying them.[4]

It can be very difficult to introduce new ways of thinking and new approaches to problems into an organization which is highly formalized. Instead it may be easier and faster to set up a new organization. The use of project groups is one way of doing this on a small scale. In government the setting up of a new department is a more drastic attempt to achieve a new approach free from a long-established departmental viewpoint.

TYPES OF FORMALIZATION

We have talked about formalization in general. Now it is useful to look at the different types so that we can examine their specific advantages and disadvantages. There are eight main types, but not all of them will be found in every organization.

1. *Rules*

This is the most common type. All, except the very smallest, organizations have rules. In some they may be written down and handed to each new employee, posted on notice boards, or included in organization manuals. In others they may be traditional rules that are well known, but have never been written down. Most people would accept the need for rules, but most would, at times, decry them as 'stupid red tape' or 'bureaucracy gone mad'. The inappropriateness of many rules, and the extent to which they are ignored, is highlighted whenever employees start 'working to rule'. The commuter who hopes to get home punctually by his usual train learns at such times what delays can be caused by working to rule.

We know all too well that rules—at least those drawn up by other people—can be stupid. We know, too, that rules can proliferate as their authors try and deal with all the different ways that people have found of getting round them. What are we to do? Abolish all rules? That is not a long-term answer though it is a way of starting afresh. The best we can do is to be aware of the dangers, to make few rules and to make them as clear as we can. We should, too, try and design rules that, as far as possible, are likely to be accepted as sensible. To achieve this it can be helpful to consult the people who are going to be asked to keep the rules.

This discussion has been of internally imposed rules, but for all organizations there are also externally imposed rules. Members of the New York Stock Exchange, for example, must operate within voluminous and stringent rules, which means that firms must perforce be highly formalized.

2. *Formal procedures*

The discussion on the advantages and disadvantages of formalization has covered all that needs to be said about formal procedures. These can be overdone, but many managers err in the other direction by paying too little attention to the need to systematize work.

3. *Organization charts*

This is a common but not a universal type of formalization, since some companies think that they can be more misleading than helpful. The usual type of chart, as in

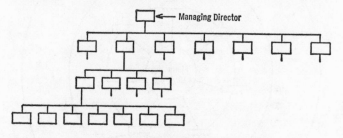

FIG. 6   Traditional organization chart

This is an abbreviated and simplified example. Many organization charts are both voluminous and complex.

Figure 6, highlights the vertical and departmental relationships, but not the horizontal ones. It gives no indication of differences in status of managers shown on the same level. It tends to show what the structure is supposed to be, rather than what it is. Also it can rapidly get out of date, and so companies that take their charts seriously have to issue new ones, or amendment sheets. In a large, rapidly changing organization this can result in a big increase in interoffice paper.

Some companies try to overcome some of the disadvantages of the traditional chart by producing one that is a different shape. A circular chart, as in Figure 7, is one of the alternatives.[5] This may be a little less misleading, but it is harder to read and it gets out of date just as quickly.

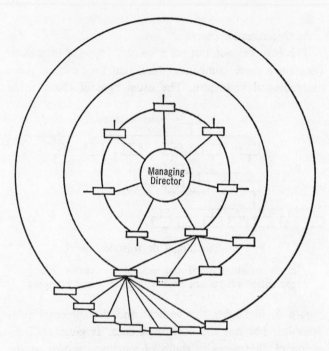

FIG. 7   Circular organization chart
(sometimes called concentric)

This contains the same information as in Figure 6,
merely arranged in a different way.

While charts have their limitations, they are still a useful tool. It would be hard to have a management succession policy in a large organization without the help of
charts. They are specially useful to the new employee, the
training department and the visiting research worker, as a
starting-point for understanding or explaining the formal
structure. Drawing up an organization chart can also help

to show up defects in the structure, and stimulate management to give more thought to how it ought to be.

4. *Organization manuals*

Organization charts are sometimes supplemented in large organizations by organization manuals. These may simply be in the form of brief notes, accompanying the departmental charts to explain the functions of each department and its relationships with other departments. At the opposite extreme they may consist of volumes which detail the responsibilities and authority of different posts and the procedures to be adopted in carrying out different tasks. Clearly the latter is only appropriate where a high degree of control is both desirable and practicable. This is true of some governmental departments.

5. *Job descriptions and job specifications*

These were discussed in Chapter 2, on division of work; they are mentioned again here because they are one of the common types of formalization.

6. *Memoranda, minutes and files*

The more formalized the organization the more communications will be written rather than spoken. Written communications provide a record that can be referred to later. This is especially important in the public service, where questions in Parliament have to be answered. It can be important, too, where the people involved do not trust each other and want to be able to refer to a record. The written word is likely to be more carefully considered than the spoken, so it encourages people to think before they write. Unfortunately they may not express themselves clearly and misunderstandings are less easily cleared up than in conversation. Written communications can take less time than spoken; it depends both on what has to be communicated and on the individuals involved.

Sometimes there is no practical choice between writing or talking—firefighting does not wait for written messages. The greater the uncertainty as to what is going to happen or what should be done, the more likely managers are to talk to each other, rather than to write.

7. *Committees*

The committee, as distinct from the informal group discussion, is one of the distinguishing features of a formalized organization. Committees can be described as discussion groups that have an agenda and which keep minutes. They may also have voluminous papers for each item on the agenda. The pros and cons of committees have already been discussed in Chapter 4 on Co-ordination.

8. *Rank and status symbols*

The more formalized an organization is the more likely it is to have formal symbols of rank and status. One purpose of these symbols is to strengthen formal authority by increasing the social distance between one level and another. There are both advantages and disadvantages in doing this, as we saw in Chapter 5 on Superior–Subordinate Relationships.

The armed services have uniforms with distinctive badges of rank. In nursing there are, or were, different uniforms for each grade of nurse and nursing officer. Industry and civil administration usually have no prescribed clothes for distinguishing ranks, but almost all have some formal rank and status symbols, apart from the informal symbols that tend to flourish. There are many examples: such as the size and furnishings of your office, what lavatories, lifts or car parks you can use. In the United States how high you are in the building is usually a reliable guide to your position in the hierarchy, but not in the United Kingdom, even in the new skyscrapers, though directors are often found at the top. In Britain how you are addressed can be important, especially in the more formalized organizations. In hospitals the nursing staff are traditionally addressed by their job: nurse, sister, matron. Attempts to drop these formal marks of rank in the nursing hierarchy can meet with strong disapproval. Sisters may object to being called Miss Brown rather than Sister: 'I have earned the title, why should I not have it?' In America the opposite applies: higher status is attached to being called Miss Brown.

9. *Appointment diaries*

A doubtful addition to the list, but perhaps worth including as another method of formalization. The ease with which one can talk to a manager, whether he is a colleague in the same company, or works for a different one, varies considerably from one organization to another. It also varies, of course, with the man's position, the more senior the man the more likely he is to have a secretary to make appointments for him. It varies too with the individual, who may have some freedom of choice. He can seek to formalize discussions with others by specifying time and duration or he can adopt an open-door policy. Organizations may make their own rules about how freely available their managers should be. There are also cultural differences. Protecting oneself with a secretary and an engagement book is a type of formalization that tends to be frowned on in the United States. In contrast, managers in some European countries attach importance to the respect that is shown by making an appointment.

Conclusion

Formalization has great advantages. Many British companies probably do not have enough of it. Managers muddle along instead of thinking how to systematize what they do. Formalization also has, as we have seen, its dangers. They are greatest when management fails to review the appropriateness of rules and procedures and the usefulness of paper work and committees. Management should frequently ask itself: 'What is the purpose of this?' Periodic spring-cleans—one of the functions of an O. & M. department—are necessary to clear away the accretions of the past: the forms that are no longer needed, the reports that no one reads, the rules that no longer apply and those that no longer should apply, the procedures that are not suited to the changed conditions and the committees that have outlived their purpose. Successful formalization needs an actively inquiring mind, one that asks 'how can we organize this best?' and one that frequently questions the current relevance of past answers.

SUMMARY

The degree of formalization is one of the scales by which organizations can be compared. A very formalized organization is one with many rules and formal procedures, and where written communication is often used in preference to spoken.

Some formalization is essential in all but the smallest organization. There must be some policies to provide for consistency in decisions and some procedures to make for smooth administration. Management's problem is to decide how much formalization is desirable.

The main advantage of formalization is that it makes for order by clarifying policy, by creating the security that comes from knowing what to expect and what to do, and by improving control. It can make for greater speed and efficiency, provided the rules and procedures are designed sensibly and not allowed to get out of date. It also ensures the equitable treatment of categories of people.

Its disadvantages are those of inflexibility. It can discourage initiative and encourages attempts to get round the rules. It can handicap adaptation to change. Rules designed to fit categories of people can cause hardship when applied to particular cases.

The main types of formalization were described with some of their advantages and disadvantages.

• • •

1. Wilfred Brown, 'What is Work?', *Harvard Business Review*, vol. 40, no. 5 (Sept–Oct 1962) p. 127. Quoted Koontz and O'Donnell, *Principles of Management*, p. 233.

2. David Granick, *The Red Executive* (London, Macmillan, 1960).

3. Melville Dalton, *Men Who Manage: Fusions of Feeling and Theory in Administration* (New York, Wiley, 1959).

4. Kaufman, *Forest Ranger*, p. 236.

5. Brech, *Organization*, pp. 436–9, describes the advantages of the circular organization chart at some length.

10 What Kind of Careers?

Management succession is a change that must take place in all organizations, even the most static ones. Managers are promoted, leave, retire or die. They have to be replaced. In some organizations this may be a haphazard process, but where management is striving to be efficient, management succession is seen as an important part of organizational planning. The aim is to provide an adequate supply of managers to fill the present and likely future needs. This chapter will discuss some of the problems of trying to do so.

The main organizational problems of management succession are:

1. To determine the numbers and types of managers likely to be needed in the future.

2. To decide what kinds of career patterns are desirable. This is such a large problem that it can be subdivided as follows:

    (a) What is the catchment group for potential managers? This is another way of asking: where should the management career ladder start? If university graduates are considered the main source of future managers, what provision should be made for other types of entrants to gain access to the management ladder?

    (b) Should any provision be made for later entrants?

(c) Should a man's career begin with experience in a technical or professional post or should it start with a more general training in the company's activities?

(d) What form of transfers or promotions between different parts of the organization are desirable and practicable?

(e) How can a man be given the kind of experience that will help to equip him to fill more senior posts successfully?

(f) Is it desirable to appoint people to top management posts when they are in their thirties or early forties?

3. To decide when organizational requirements are more important than individual needs and vice versa.

This list does not include many of the problems that must be considered in trying to provide the future management; problems such as how to select the most suitable candidates for a position, how to assess potential, what kind of training to provide, and so on. These problems, and many others, would need to be discussed if the subject was management selection and development, but our discussion is limited to the organizational problems of management succession.

DETERMINING FUTURE MANAGEMENT NEEDS

In the foreseeable future how many and what kinds of managers are likely to be needed? This is a question that should be considered in any continuing organization. Is the organization likely to expand, to remain the same size or to contract? Can any estimate be made of the likely size of the expansion or contraction? Management may say that it is impossible to predict, or even to try to estimate, what the likely size and shape of the organization will be in five years' time, far less in twenty years' time. Yet the recruitment of potential managers will be based on some assumptions about this, even if these are not made explicit. The larger the company the more true this will be because of the numbers involved.

These are relatively straightforward questions, although they may be hard to answer. It is more difficult to decide what assumptions should be made about the future composition of management. Is it reasonable to assume that the organization is likely to remain the same shape, so that the same proportions of managers as before are needed at each level of management? The traditional management hierarchy is pyramid-shaped, so that many more junior managers are needed than middle managers and many fewer top managers than middle managers. There are indications that this traditional shape may change, and there are already some examples of companies where this is happening, with a decrease in lower-level jobs and an increase at the middle-management level.

Changes in the technical and professional composition of management provide another tricky problem for management succession planning. Even if a company gets its estimates of numbers right, it may still be badly wrong about the type of people who are required. The problem of the right mix of professional and technical skills is much greater in an organization that needs many managers with this kind of background than it is for a commercial or administrative organization where most recruits can be

of undifferentiated management potential. The right mix
is usually thought of in terms of technical and professional
qualifications, but the right mix of abilities can also be
important. It is unusual for organizations to attempt to recruit for different levels of managerial potential. Most set
a minimum level of academic attainment and above that
select the best candidates they can get instead of deliberately aiming at a range of abilities. As McClelland has
said: 'This situation can be tolerated only so long as the
predictive value of selection procedures remains so low.'[1]
He pointed out that in the absence of a rapid turnover
there are large differences in the ultimate extent of promotion of entrants selected on similar criteria.

CAREER PATTERNS FOR MANAGEMENT

Planning career patterns for different types of entrants
is part of a policy for management succession. Such planning can also be used as evidence that the company has
a career policy. So many organizations are now competing
for the better graduates that young men expect to know
what their career prospects are likely to be, at least in the
short term. They will rarely be satisfied with general ref-
erences to 'unlimited scope' or 'the future is up to you',
and very sensibly too, because in a large organization it
is easy to get overlooked. One must be promoted sufficiently rapidly in the early years if one is to be in the run-
ning for top jobs later. In large organizations there must
be a system for checking on how career planning is working out in practice.

Where should the management career ladder start? The
traditional answer was: 'at the bottom—come in on the

shop floor or in the office and work your way up to the top'. In large organizations this is much rarer today, and is likely to become rarer still. Most of them are now looking to the university graduate and the later school-leaver for their potential managers. This is where the management ladder tends to start. There may still be bridges provided from the non-managerial career ladders, but in a large organization there may be too many rungs to be climbed for the apprentice or junior clerk to have much chance of reaching the top. The existence of professional and technical requirements for management posts is also an important limitation to promotion from the bottom. Hospital domestic staff cannot rise to become matrons, nor is the laboratory assistant likely to be able to technically qualify himself by spare-time study for the position of chief chemist in a large company. A still greater barrier than lack of formal qualifications is the time needed to climb up a long ladder when others started higher up.

Few large companies aim to recruit people over 30; sometimes 25 is the limit. There are some specialist posts for which they may have to do so, as the internal supply is inadequate or nonexistent, but few do so because they believe that they should have some later entrants. There are two arguments in favour. One is that they can bring new ideas from their experience in other organizations. The other is that they can be a source of able managers rather than just of potential managers as in the case of younger entrants. The arguments against this policy are that it reduces promotion opportunities for existing staff and that the newcomers may find it hard to adjust to the managerial climate.

There is a sharp policy division between those who believe in recruiting a potential manager direct into a specific job, and those who think that he should first be shown something of the range of the organization's activities. Both policies have their advantages and disadvantages. The former has the merit of giving the new recruit something that he can do from the beginning and, if he has a relevant qualification, an opportunity to use this. It also means that he can be immediately useful. Against this it is hard to find something useful for a graduate with no specialist qualification to do that is sufficiently demanding for him. Another disadvantage is that the man can rapidly become rather specialized, so that later the company may have to try and correct the limitations of too narrow an outlook. The disadvantage of the other method—of moving the new recruit around—is that he may get bored, unless his tour of different departments is well planned and he is given something constructive to do. A further snag is that the man is a cost rather than an asset during this time and may leave the company before he has made any contribution. However, this may well be the easiest time to show him a wide range of the organization's work. It provides an opportunity not only for the man to see which aspect of the organization's work interests him most, but also for different managers to see the new recruits and decide whom they would like to have in their department.

An important and difficult decision that has to be made about career patterns is how narrow or broad they should be in terms of the organization's main activities. The traditional career pattern was for the young recruit to go into one department and to be promoted solely within it. This gave him a good knowledge of that department's work and helped to develop strong departmental loyalties. The advantages were also the disadvantages. A man who has spent his whole career in one department is likely to know little of the work of other departments and may find it difficult to understand their problems and point of view. His dominant loyalty may be to the department rather than to the company, so that in disputes with other departments he may be likely to put his department's interests first. There is also the important disadvantage that promotion solely within one department is poor preparation for top management where an appreciation of all aspects of the business is desirable.

The advantages of gaining experience in different parts of the organization are increasingly recognized. However, it is one thing to say that it is a good idea for a man to have such experience, another to try and plan his career so that he can get it. The more specialist different departments are, the harder it is to transfer somebody who has not had the specialist training. Interchange between departments is usually easier in some occupations than in others. Some, such as electrical engineers in steel works, have expertise which can be used in a number of departments. Others may have a technical background that is only useful in one. Jobs in central service departments are used by some companies as useful training posts for young graduates because they bring their holders into contact with a number of different departments.

Transfers between departments is one way of providing wider job experience. It is often the most difficult to arrange. Transfers between different locations is another type of job mobility which is used by many large companies that are geographically dispersed. Often, as in banking, it may be the only way to get promotion. The value of this kind of mobility is that it can help to prevent too parochial an outlook. Its main disadvantage is its social cost.

An aspect of transfers that is often overlooked is the effect that these can have on the pattern of loyalties in the company. Who does the manager think of as 'we'; is it his department, the division, a subsidiary company, or the company as a whole? A man who spends a long time in one department or in one local establishment is likely to identify with that. His loyalty to it may be stronger than to the organization as a whole. Career planning should take into account the kind of loyalties that managers should be encouraged to develop.

The planning of career patterns should be based on a good understanding of the different types of jobs in the company and of the kind of experience that they offer. Such understanding is often all too limited. Most training managers think of jobs as being either junior, middle or top management, and perhaps also as belonging to one of the main functions, but not of other differences. There is too little analysis of the nature of different jobs in the organization and of the ways in which experience in these jobs may help or hinder a man's development.[2] Both Wilson and McClelland have pointed out the different skills that may be required at different levels. This can mean that the skills developed at one level can even be a disqualification for promotion to another where quite different skills are required. Wilson cites the difference between the skills needed at junior levels in financial or commercial departments and those needed in the more senior posts. At the junior levels what is required is patience, accuracy and tolerance of routine. A little higher up, the safeguarding of assets may be an important activity, but at the top, as Wilson says:

> the main responsibility is almost the opposite of passive safeguarding of assets; it is that of trying actively to increase the assets by making estimates of probability and by sharing decisions about complex risk-taking, the organized 'gambling', which makes up such an important proportion of top management work. A man who may well have considerable potential for this high-level work may be seriously handicapped if he spends more than a short period of his career in the routine-dominated lower levels where the primary responsibilities are of a quite different character.[3]

McClelland points out the difference in the skills required at different levels in marketing:

> It is natural to recruit marketing directors from sales managers who in turn are often former sales representatives. Their earlier experience, therefore, has been in the arts of enthusiastic persuasion. To convince others one must convince oneself, and in many sales forces criticisms of the product, or an other than optimistic assessment of its sales potential, would be dysfunctional and therefore regarded as disloyal. Yet a marketing director must be highly realistic in his appraisals, and highly critical of new products: attitudes which require a switch through 180° from those which have had to become second nature to him at an earlier stage.[4]

The author has noticed similar differences in different levels of works management. The more junior and middle levels of production management usually require both good man management and the ability to deal rapidly with a large number of different queries and minor crises. The job is a very episodic one, and so the manager has little opportunity to plan. Too long a time in such a job may make it hard for him to adjust to the demands of a more senior post where he should devote more time and effort to planning. The change from a job that requires a man to respond to others, to one where he has to spend more time planning can be difficult. Many works managers, and hospital matrons too, may try and evade the problem by spending long hours on inspection. Former bank managers may find the same difficulty when they are promoted to a divisional or head office. 'It was dreadful,' said one, 'there I was in a room by myself with lots of papers. Nobody came to see me and the telephone rarely rang.'

It needs to be recognized that some jobs are much better for training future top management than others. Lucky is the organization that has a number of small units where a young manager can have experience of independent command of different functions. In monolithic large organizations it is hard to find any satisfactory substitute for this sort of experience. Most of the junior and middle-management jobs are likely to be specialist jobs in one particular function. Such jobs neither prepare the incumbent for the broader approach of top management, nor for its uncertainties. Some of these uncertainties surround the decisions that have to be made, others come from the 'intensely personal nature of top management'—to use the tactful phrase of an American research group.[5] The opportunity to practise general management at a young age, in a setting where mistakes will not be too costly, is one valuable form of training. Another is working in a job that brings the young man into close touch with top management. Such a job has the advantage that it enables him to observe something of the nature of top management work; it also has a more personal advantage, that it makes him visible to top management.

In a much-quoted paper, Leavitt and Whisler predicted that electronic data processing would make it still harder to provide potential top managers with relevant experience since the work of middle managers would become much more routine.[6] There seems so far little evidence that this prediction will prove to be correct. At present the more advanced uses of the computer pose a different kind of problem, that top management may not have the training to understand what is being done and must rely on the advice of their subordinates. Of course, they have often had to do so before, but this is a major new area of ignorance. This ignorance may be a temporary phase, as those with a knowledge of computers reach top management posts.

'The average age of our executive directors is 41.' Even large organizations may make such a claim. New and smaller ones may boast of a still younger top management. In many organizations people are being appointed to top posts at an earlier age than in the past. This it is urged helps to keep top management up to date and stops able young men from being frustrated. True, but it can pose severe problems later on. Unless the organization is a rapidly expanding one the top posts may be blocked for twenty years or more. It can be hard, too, to retain enthusiasm and initiative if one is in the same job for so long. A suggested solution is a switch to a completely different career long before retirement. Good in theory, perhaps, but there are not many examples in practice. Meanwhile the problem is likely to become more evident as the present young top managers get older.

Finally, we should remember that promotion is the main way of rewarding exceptional talent. This common assumption about career patterns can cause difficulties. In a world of increasingly complex specialities it may make it difficult to reward adequately a man with exceptional professional skill and still let him continue to practise that skill. Yet as McClelland points out:

> There is no inevitability about the roles superior in the hierarchy being preferable, even in terms of remuneration, to those lower down. Highly skilled work such as teaching or healing or doing research or providing entertainment may properly attract higher rewards than the administration of it. Outside business this is not revolutionary doctrine and even inside business the need to employ professional specialists of various sorts may result in such doctrine appearing less outrageous in a few years time than it does now.[7]

BALANCING THE NEEDS OF JOBS AND PEOPLE

All large organizations are to a greater or lesser extent bureaucratic. This means that they consist of posts which continue when their holder leaves, thus making for continuity.[8] In a very bureaucratic organization the job specification, which describes the kind of person who should fill the vacant job, will be very precisely laid down. So also may be the categories of employees who are entitled to be considered for the post. The job specification is likely to be more detailed for jobs that have existed for some time than for new jobs, where the requirements are not yet as clearly known. In a less bureaucratic organization more attention will be paid to the particular abilities and characteristics of the possible successors and the jobs may be altered to take account of their special strengths or weaknesses. This is most likely to happen in small organizations where a limited supply of good people may make it imperative to use their abilities to the full.

People vary. Different people, even if they have a similar background, training and ability, may do the same job in different ways. There is—fortunately for us diverse human beings—no one recipe for a good manager. We know that even in highly bureaucratic organizations, like the armed services, officers can differ in the way they do a particular job. People can mould the job to some extent, however detailed the job description. Their opportunities for doing so are likely to be greater in the more senior jobs, where the nature of the work can be less clearly defined than in the more junior jobs.

A new managing director may well spend his time differently from his predecessor, so that although the title and the responsibilities remain the same, what he is actually doing may well be very different. This is most likely where the new man has a different functional background from his predecessor. A change in the way the managing director divides his time between different activities will also have repercussions on the work of his immediate subordinates.

One of the conclusions of an American study of top-management development and succession was that:

The distinctions between job description and man description break down at the upper management levels. The man-in-the-job emerges as a single concept.[9]

The authors also conclude that:

An adequate philosophy of management development cannot concentrate exclusively on manipulation of the individual by selection, appraisal and training. Several companies among the thirteen studied made organizational changes to mould a position to the man assigned. This was not considered merely an improvisation to meet contingencies, but a desirable practice. Management organizations are structured around people.[10]

The development needs of an individual may conflict with the short-term view of organizational efficiency. An individual may be ready for a change of job but there may be no suitable vacancy. Should he have to wait until there is one or should a vacancy be made for him? Usually managers have to wait, but some companies say that they create opportunities for the people considered to be fliers. Another conflict is between the time a man needs to gain useful experience in a job and the often, much longer period, that is needed to get over the learning period and to make a useful contribution. The organization's short-term needs will sometimes have to be sacrificed so that a potential top manager can be promoted fast enough for him to reach the top before he has to retire.

SUMMARY

There are three main organizational problems in providing for management succession. The first is determining how many and what kinds of managers will be needed in the future. In a large organization some assumptions about this must be made, either explicitly or implicitly, when recruiting. The second problem is deciding what kind of career patterns are desirable. This requires decisions about the type of career ladders that should exist. Where should the management ladder start? What provisions can and should be made for those who start on a more junior ladder to get on to the managerial one? Is it desirable to encourage transfers from one ladder to another? If so, what transfers are practicable and when should they be made? Should a man's career begin with a general training in the activities of the organization or in a specific post? The advantages and disadvantages of different policies are discussed. It is urged that management development officers should know enough about each kind of job in their organization to understand what type of experience it provides. Some junior- and middle-management jobs require qualities that are the opposite of those needed in senior posts in the same function.

The third organizational problem is to strike the balance between selecting individuals for specific well-defined jobs and adapting jobs to individuals. The extent to which jobs can be changed to accommodate individuals varies with the management level, with the size of the organization, and with the extent to which it is bureaucratic. Very large organizations are likely to be more rigid than smaller ones. But even in large organizations there is more flexibility at the top than lower down. Career planning, particularly for those judged to have high potential, may mean balancing short-term organizational needs against possible long-term advantages.

.   .   .

1. W. G. McClelland, 'Career Patterns and Organizational Needs', in R. J. Hacon (ed.), *Organizational Necessities and Individual Needs* (A.T.M. Occasional Papers, no. 5, Sept 1968. Oxford, Blackwell) p. 26.

2. This point is argued in more detail in the author's *Managers and their Jobs,* chap. 7.

3. A. T. M. Wilson, 'Some Sociological Aspects of Systematic Management Development', in R. J. Hacon (ed.), *Organizational Necessities and Individual Needs.*

4. McClelland, 'Career Patterns and Organizational Needs', p. 29.

5. Albert S. Glickman, Clifford Hahn, Edwin A. Fleishman and Brent Baxtern, *Top Management Development and Succession* (Supplementary Paper No. 27, The Committee for Economic Development, N.Y., 1968) p. 9.

6. Leavitt and Whisler, 'Management in the 1980s'.

7. McClelland, 'Career Patterns and Organizational Needs', p. 31.

8. For a longer discussion of the characteristics of bureaucracies see Stewart, *The Reality of Management,* chap. 1.

9. Glickman *et al., Top Management Development and Succession,* p. 10.

10. Ibid., p. 3.

11 The Changing Organization

Organizations are not islands that can live unto themselves, ignoring the world around them. They are shaped by their environment and also help to shape it. The purpose of this chapter is to look at this interaction and to try and understand the ways in which organizations are changing.

EXTERNAL CHANGES AFFECTING ORGANIZATIONS

Growth of state intervention
The increase in state intervention is one of the most striking changes affecting companies though it affects other organizations too. It is important now, but also has a long history as governments have concerned themselves more and more with what industry and commerce are doing. Today, every facet of a business's activities may be affected by government regulations. In the very large company it is not only the regulations that affect management's action, but also the threat of new regulations that may influence management decisions.

The amount of government intervention has increased. It has also changed its character. Initially Western governments were primarily concerned with establishing the rules within which businesses should operate. This has been described as 'holding the ring'. Now many governments are also concerned with the management process itself. The British Government, confronted with years of balance-of-payments crises, sought for means by which it could improve the efficiency of industry and stimulate exports. Its efforts ranged from honours for exporters to providing the finance to encourage the amalgamation of companies in the hope that bigger units would be able to compete more effectively in the international market.

An important by-product of these new forms of government intervention has been the growing involvement of individual businessmen in such government efforts. Many top managers now have less time than in the past to devote to their own companies. Much of their time is spent on government advisory committees, taking part in committees and boards for their industry or even being seconded to government departments.

2. *Growth of trade union intervention*

The most important recent change in trade union activities that affects organizations is the extension of trade unionism to new classes of workers. The growth of white-collar trade unions, covering a wide variety of occupations and the increasing militancy of some professional associations, has changed the connotation of 'staff'. In the past many managements thought of them as having a much greater loyalty to the organization than manual workers. Now the relationship has become a more contractual one. The idea that teachers, doctors, bank clerks or airline pilots might strike is one that managers and administrators in different parts of the world have now had to accept.

Governments, trade unions and professional associations are the main types of intervention in the internal affairs of other organizations. Another form of organized intervention, that of the consumer, is foreseeable but so far has had little influence. However, with the establishment of consumers' and patients' associations there is more activity than there used to be.

3. *Rapid technical change*

The rapid rate of technical change has altered the tempo of the environment within which organizations must live. To survive in this rapidly changing world they must adapt faster. This is true, for example, of the Health Service where advances in medical knowledge and equipment are bringing changing patterns of patient care.

One of the main impacts of technical change on companies is the high rate of product obsolescence. In the past if a company developed a good product it could expect to go on selling it for many years. Now few products are invulnerable to the effects of technical change, hence many companies must devote increasingly large sums to research and development. Material substitution may change the character of an industry or make it obsolete. The development of new products may replace others as television has partly replaced the cinema.

4. *One world*

This is not true politically but it is increasingly true culturally and commercially. China is so far the big exception. Fast transport and world-wide communications reduce cultural differences. Increasingly cities look like each other, and so do the clothes and transport of the people who live in them. What they eat and drink differs more, but some brand products are found in every continent, Coca Cola, Schweppes Tonic and Gordon's Gin among them.

The growth of a world-wide market is taking place in a world in which more and more countries are becoming independent nations and wanting to control their own economy. Companies operating from overseas are viewed with suspicion in many countries. Selling in a foreign market now often means establishing a subsidiary there. This introduces new management problems for companies that had previously operated only from their home base.

5. *More educated population*

This has had two repercussions for organizations. One, it has raised workers' expectations. A better-educated worker can offer more; he also expects more. He expects to be treated as a person rather than as a hand. This has had its influence on managerial style, and has, together with full employment, contributed to a decline in autocratic management. Two, the higher proportion of the population going to universities has forced more organizations to go to them for at least some of their potential managers. This has raised the recruitment age for this group and has posed problems of fitting them in. The university graduate has higher expectations than the school-leaver, but is not necessarily immediately more useful. He is also in a better position to move elsewhere if he is not satisfied than were recruits in earlier years. The competition for the abler graduates has made large organizations take more effort both to attract and to retain them. A good management development scheme with well-thought-out and well-explained, career opportunities has become one of the ways of doing so.

6. *Full employment*

The changes described so far affect organizations in many countries. The impact of full employment is more limited as fewer countries have had full employment continuously since the war. It has affected personnel policies and the relations between superiors and subordinates since the threat of the sack is now often not a practical way of supporting one's authority.

These six major changes alter the environment within which organizations must operate. Their main impact is on companies, but others are affected too. The nature of the changes taking place in organizations, partly or wholly as a result of these environmental changes, are described below.

CHANGES WITHIN ORGANIZATIONS

1. *Increasing size*

This is the most striking change that is taking place in companies in different parts of the world. The proportion of assets, for example, owned by the top 500 companies in the United States and the United Kingdom is constantly increasing. Nor is there any sign that this trend towards larger organizations will slow down. The threat of acquisition, which exists for all but the very largest companies, is likely to remain. It has become greater in some United Kingdom industries as a result of government intervention aimed at creating units that are large enough to com-

pete with their American rivals. American competition is
a worry for other European nations, too, which may lead
to more defensive mergers of companies in different European countries.

There are four main advantages for companies in being
large: in a technical industry it is easier to finance the
necessary research and development to keep pace with,
or ahead of, competitors in the search for improved products; in many industries there are economies to be achieved
by large-scale production; increasingly, with the growth
of a world market, there are economies too, to be gained
by a larger selling base; and, finally, there is the defensive
advantage that one is less likely to be taken over.

The increase in size is most marked in business and
government service, but it is also found elsewhere. Farms
are becoming larger, so are hospitals and schools. The
large new district general hospitals in Britain are due, at
least in part, to the increasing cost of medical services.
Larger hospitals can more economically support the range
of medical services that are needed.

We have talked about the advantages of increasing size,
but we all know that there are many disadvantages too.
The problems of organization become more complex and
take up more of management's time. It is harder to achieve
the right balance between order and flexibility or between
centralization and decentralization. Human relations problems tend to be greater in large organizations. Increasing
size is often necessary for economic reasons, but in many
ways it makes managers' lives more difficult.

2. *The growth of the international corporation*

Before the war, oil companies were the main international corporations. Now companies in other industries are having to become both more internationally-minded and more international. The development of a world-wide consumer market has opened up new opportunities for expansion, so has the international market for advanced technical equipment. The domestic market of medium-sized countries like Britain is no longer large enough to support the cost of research and development in highly technical industries such as computers and aero engines. Both must have foreign markets if they are to hope to pay their way.

There have been international trading companies for centuries and companies that marketed their products abroad. What is new is the great increase in the number of subsidiary and associated companies overseas, as well as the development of multi-national companies. Now even medium-sized companies may have their overseas subsidiaries to manufacture and sell their products. Local regulations may make this a prerequisite to selling their goods in that country.

In the past overseas subsidiaries were often run by expatriate managers. This is changing rapidly as more and more governments are saying that foreign managers must be replaced by their own nationals. The training of local replacements for expatriate managers, is one of the transitional tasks of management development in international companies.

The growth of the international corporation changes the way in which its managers think. Strategic thinking can be done world-wide. This makes the task of trying to optimize resources much more complex. Here operational research can help, backed up by large computers, so managers need to be more numerate. They need, too, an understanding of local politics and a sensitivity to cultural differences if they are to operate successfully in other countries. The oil companies have known this for a long time and, by virtue of this international approach, have seemed to be in a different class in their management thinking from other industries. Now more and more companies are having to learn the same lessons.

3. *More fluid boundaries*

The main effect of the environmental changes, which we described, is to make the boundaries of the organization more fluid—that is, to make it less autonomous. Organizations, particularly those in business, are now much more subject to external influences than they were in the years before the last war. This means that management must be able to adjust faster than in the past. To do so requires both a greater sensitivity to what is happening in the world outside and a more flexible organization.

Many more people in the organization have boundary roles than in the interwar period. Then, it was primarily the sales department which had to deal with people both inside and outside the company. Now many managers in other departments will also have external contacts. The fact that top managers may spend much of their time with people from outside the organization is a reflection of the importance of the environment to its success.

4. *Changes in staff composition*

The relative proportions of different types of staff have altered in many organizations. There are far more knowledge workers, while automation has often decreased the number of manual and clerical workers. The result is a change in the shape of the traditional organizational pyramid with many more people at the intermediate levels and fewer at the bottom. The problem of many managers is now that of managing specialists rather than that of managing manual workers.

5. *Increasing job specialization and professionalization*

This is a particular aspect of the changes in the composition of staff. Rapid technical change has produced new specialities and led to the further subdivision of existing ones. It has also meant that a man's technical knowledge gets out of date much faster than in the past. We saw in Chapter 6 on The Manager and the Specialist that the manager's job has changed as a result. The result of these changes is a less formal hierarchy, more time spent in discussions with colleagues, and more informal, democratic relations between superior and subordinate.

Professionalization has changed the reference-point for many employees. They look to their professional peers for judgement on their activities and often expect to get their promotion by moving to another company. Their loyalty is to their profession rather than to their employer.

6. *Changes in career patterns*

Five factors are changing career patterns: the increasing size of organizations, the larger number of international companies, the growth of specialization and professionalization, full employment, and the growing concern about the standard of management efficiency. The last one was not included in the four environmental changes described earlier, as it may be partly, or wholly, a by-product of them. But it is worth mentioning separately here as it has helped to make people pay more attention to career planning.

Some large organizations have an extra dimension in their career planning, that of providing the experience that will help future top management to think internationally. The parent company may take as one of its most important responsibilities that of ensuring good management for its subsidiaries throughout the world. This will mean both world-wide career planning for top-management and world-wide management training. Much of it can be done in the national's home country, but companies like Shell and Unilever also bring their managers to England for special training, as well as sending them to courses in other countries.

Career patterns are changed by increasing specialization. New careers open up, as in management science. These pose problems of recruitment, training and of integration into the existing career structure. Increasing specialization can make career paths narrower and job mobility more difficult. The danger is a myopic view of the organization. To avoid this there must be more formal management development and career planning. Many managers will come from the ranks of the specialists. This can pose special training problems, as specialists often find it hard to think like managers.

Full employment has increased the competition for good men—and, to a much smaller extent, for good women. This has encouraged job mobility, as a man who thinks he is not getting on well enough in one organization can often, particularly if he is under forty, try his luck in another. One result of this is that people are getting to top management, as we saw in the last chapter, at a younger stage.

7. Decline in hierarchical differences

Enough has already been said in Chapter 5 (Superior–Subordinate Relationships) about the reasons for this and they are also indicated in the following table. We should not underrate the importance of this change in affecting relationships between superiors and subordinates and in influencing the channels of communication. In a very hierarchical organization communication is mainly up and down. In a more informal, organic, organization much more takes place horizontally. More, too, is spoken, whereas in the very hierarchical organization written communications are more common.

Table 1 shows the relationships between the six environmental changes that we described and the changes that have taken place in organizations. The relationships between the two should be thought of as interacting, so that although the changes in organizations are due, in whole or in part, to the changes in the environment, some of the changes in organizations also have repercussions in the environment. Rapid technical change, for example, has helped to produce organizations like I.B.M., but the company has also contributed, through its research, to technical change. The international corporation stems from the growth of one world, from rapid technological change, and from government intervention, which may make it profitable for the corporation to adjust its profits to the tax laws of different countries and even to change its head office. But the increasing scale of companies has also brought more government intervention to restrict their power.

TABLE I The impact of changes in the environment on changes in organizations

Changes in environment ↓	Resulting changes in organisation						
	Increasing size	Growth of international corporations	More fluid boundaries	Changing composition of Staff	Increasing job specialization and professionalization	Changing career patterns	Less hierarchical differentiation
Intervention by State	Yes	Yes	Yes	–	–	–	–
Intervention by trade union and professional associations	–	–	Yes	–	Yes	–	–
Rapid technical change	Yes	Yes	Yes	Yes	Yes	Yes	Yes
One world	Yes	Yes	–	–	–	Yes	–
More educated population	–	–	Yes	Yes	Yes	Yes	Yes
Full employment	–	–	Yes	Yes	–	Yes	Yes

Not all the organizational changes that we have described have taken place in every organization. Large companies in highly technical industries are likely to have been most affected. Let us look at how many of these changes have taken place in one large company, International Computers Ltd, the largest computer company in the United Kingdom. Briefly, the history of this company is that it was created by successive mergers. The first was in 1959 between Power-Samas and British Tabulating Machines, two punched-card machine companies. This merger, like the second one, took place primarily in order to pool research costs and to be in a stronger position to meet United States' competition. The new company, I.C.T. (International Computers and Tabulators), found it difficult to compete successfully with I.B.M., the huge American computer company. The Ministry of Technology, through the Industrial Expansion Act, promoted a merger in 1968 between I.C.T. and the computer division of English Electric, the other main British computer manufacturer, and now has a 10.5 per cent shareholding in the resultant company, I.C.L.

External changes	*Affected I.C.L. or, earlier, its constituent companies?*
State intervention	Yes, both in the ways in which other companies are affected, through taxation and government regulations, and through the Ministry of Technology's encouragement of the merger between I.C.T. and English Electric.
Trade union intervention	Yes, but in general only, nothing special to the company.

Rapid technical change	Yes, it was the rapidity and cost-liness of technical change in this industry which was the main reason for the mergers. It has also affected the jobs within the organization. The change-over from punched cards to computers created more spe-cialized and highly technical jobs.
One world	Yes, the growing market for com-puters in different countries meant greater opportunities and more international compe-tition as companies needed to have a larger market base to support their research.
	Technical staff would have to be located in the potential sales areas, both to sell and then to service.
	Even so, the impact on I.C.L. is probably less than in a consumer-goods company since technical companies have for a long time expected to sell some of their output overseas.
More educated population	Yes⎱
	⎰but nothing special to I.C.L.
Full employment	Yes⎰

Now let us look at the consequential organizational changes in the company.

Organizational changes	*Affected I.C.L. or, earlier, its constituent companies?*
Increasing size	Yes, primarily as a result of the mergers.

International corporation	Yes, in order to compete successfully I.C.L. has had overseas subsidiaries for many years.
More fluid boundaries	Yes, as in all companies, and especially the larger ones.
Change in the staff composition	Little change as the company, and its predecessors, have always had relatively more people of higher levels than many manufacturing companies.
Increasing job specialization	Yes, to a greater extent than companies in less technical industries, particularly specialized sales areas are matched to customers' specific requirements.
Changes in career patterns	Probably more opportunities for specialists to get into management. An increase in the standard of people required.
Less hierarchical organization	A company which started, as the constituent companies did, in a technical industry, is unlikely to have been very hierarchical at any stage in its history.

The example chosen is one that would show more change than many other manufacturing companies, and even more than other types of organization. Yet if we look at a very different type of organization—a general hospital in England—we will also be able to trace the effects of environmental changes.

| *External changes* | *Affected the general hospital?* |
| State intervention | Yes, most markedly through the introduction of the National Health Service and the resulting changes in the ownership and organization of hospitals. |

Intervention by trade unions and professional associations	Trade union intervention is now increasing in the Health Service, so are the activities of professional associations.
Rapid technical change	Yes, primarily through medical advances and the development of new equipment. These are a major factor in the increasing size of general hospitals and in the greater specialization of patient care through the establishment of intensive care units.
One world	Yes, through the large number of foreign staff now employed and their short periods of service with hospitals in the United Kingdom.
More educated population	Yes, but nothing that is special to a general hospital.
Full employment	Yes, because of relatively low salaries, which have made it harder both to attract and retain good staff.
Organizational changes	*Affected the general hospital?*
Increasing size	Yes, through the establishment of the large district general hospitals, and the closure of smaller hospitals.
International corporation	Not applicable.
More fluid boundaries	Yes, as a result of the activities of the Department of Health and Social Security, the Regional Hospital Boards, and the numerous committees of inquiry, as well as more community pressures. The role of the hospital has also changed to one that is more community-

	oriented, and where patterns of care change rapidly.
Change in staff composition	Yes, as a result of recommendations from various inquiries and reviews.
Increasing job specialization	Yes, both in medicine and by the addition of new specialist staff on the administrative side, such as operational research and catering officers.
Changes in career patterns	Yes, much more attention being paid to planning careers, and more interchange between hospitals.
Less hierarchical organization	Yes, to a small extent, amongst nursing staff where, within a continuing strong hierarchy, there are rather more permissive attitudes, more discussions and a decrease in status symbols.

SUMMARY

This chapter has sought to trace the changes in the environment that have affected organizations. These are: the growth of state and trade union intervention, rapid technical change, the breaking down of cultural and commercial distinctions between nations, a more educated population and full employment.

The impact of these changes was summarized in Table 1 (p. 197). It shows that rapid technical change has had the most widespread repercussions.

The increasing size of organizations is stimulated by state intervention, by rapid technical change and by the opportunities of world-wide markets. International corporations have developed for the same reasons. One of the most striking changes in organizations is the extent to which their boundaries with the outside world have become more fluid as a result of external pressures. Then there may be a number of staff changes. There are more knowledge workers and fewer people in manual and junior clerical grades. Jobs are more specialized. Career patterns have changed and are still changing. There are less strongly marked differences between hierarchical levels as relations between superior and subordinate have been affected by rapid technical change, a higher level of education and full employment.

12 What Can Go Wrong?

Any organization needs to be reviewed periodically to see that it is still appropriate for current needs. This is true both of the organization as a whole and of its individual parts. When doing so it is useful to remember some of the common mistakes that can be made in setting up organizations or that can develop with time. This chapter is intended as a brief guide to these mistakes. The questions can be used as a check-list to help expose particular mistakes.

1. *What objectives have been set? Do these cover all the main aspects of the organization?*

The need to be clear about one's objectives has become almost a cliché. Yet any list of common mistakes must still start with it.

There are two dangers: one is that only lip service will be paid to the need, the other is that what is meant by objectives can be too general to be a useful guide to planning. In business it is not sufficient to say that one's objective is to make a profit, as that leaves so many questions unanswered. Nor is it sufficient in hospitals to say that one's aim is to care for patients. What is needed is a series of objectives, covering each of the main areas of the organization's activities. In a company these will include among others: the amount of profit; the level of productivity; and the kind of markets that it wants to serve and the standing it is aiming for in those markets.

Only when management has defined its objectives for the different areas can it decide what is likely to be the best form of organization to meet them. For example, does the company aim to offer after-sales service? If it does, it will need a different form of organization from one that does not do so. Is the aim to expand sales overseas? A company that provides after-sales service will have to think twice before selling in new areas.

Common mistake: Failing to start all organizational planning by asking, 'What are the aims?' Questions about what is the most efficient form of organization are meaningless unless this is done.

2. *Is the form of organization suitable for the environment in which it has to operate?*

If the objectives have been well thought out this question should be superfluous. Yet it is worth including as an additional check on one's thinking.

Research has shown us that the form of organization should vary with the situation with which it has to deal. One of the most important variables is the rate of change in the environment. Where an organization is exposed to a very rapid rate of change it will need to be much more flexible than if it operates in stable conditions. This has a bearing on the degree of formalization of procedures and responsibilities that will be appropriate.

Common mistake: Designing an organization with too little thought for the environment in which it has to operate.

3. *In the last few years how have the aims or circumstances of the organization changed? What are the*

implications of these changes for the type of structure?

It is easy to let one's objectives get out of date and hence fail to adapt the organization to changing needs. For example, one may continue, as many companies do, with the same recruitment and promotion policies long after changes in the labour market have made them inappropriate. Large-scale employers need to be particularly aware of changes in the composition of the population and in educational and social patterns, such as the proportion of school-leavers going on to university, the average age of marriage and childbirth, and the size of the average family, as these may all have implications for recruitment policies.

Some changes, such as mergers, naturally stimulate managers to think about organization. Other changes take place without managers being fully aware of them or of the resulting need to adapt the organization. Firms that are used to a sellers' market are often slow to adjust to a swing to a buyers' market, requiring a much more active sales policy and, perhaps, a larger and more decentralized sales organization.

Common mistake: Continuing with a form of organization that is no longer suitable.

4. *Which decisions are most vital to success?*
   Who is taking these decisions?

Top management ought to determine which decisions are most important for success. These are the ones on which it should take the final decision. The danger is that top management will not have sought to identify the decisions that matter most, or that even if it has it will not spend the time necessary to give them adequate attention.

Common mistake: Top management preoccupied with details and matters of secondary importance instead of concentrating on the most vital decisions.

5. *Which decisions should be taken by those who have to implement them?*

There is much to be said for the view that decisions should be taken at the lowest level that is practicable. In Chapter 8 on Decentralization we saw some of the factors that affect what is practicable, and noted that these may vary at different stages of development. Many decisions are likely to be better if they are taken by those who know the local conditions and the people who will be affected. There are, of course, others that will be better for the wider perspective that a more senior man should be able to bring to the problem. Pushing decisions as far down in the hierarchy as possible makes junior jobs more interesting—the intention behind the job-enrichment policies that some companies are now pursuing. The implementation of decisions is also likely to be better as people will usually be more motivated to carry out their own decisions than those of others.

Management may fail to decentralize because it has not analysed the nature of the decisions nor where they ought to be taken. Often managers may take too many decisions themselves because they are reluctant to delegate.

Common mistake: Failing to realize which decisions are better taken at a lower level, or reluctance to delegate.

6. *Is the grouping of activities satisfactory?*

Any organization is divided into departments which bring together related types of work, but it is often a problem to decide what activities should be put together. In Chapter 3 on Grouping we looked at the different bases that can be used, such as product, function or location, and saw that each had its advantages and disadvantages. It is important to consider what arrangement gives the best balance between them. Like other organizational decisions, it is one that needs to be reviewed periodically. Is it, for example, still best to organize the sales force by areas with the area salesmen selling all products, or is there now a greater need for more specialized salesmen? If so, the sales department would need to be reorganized into different product groups. A decision that frequently needs reviewing is the location of particular specialist activities. Some activities, such as the laundry in hospitals, may now more economically be operated as a central service. Others may need to be decentralized to the operating units.

Common mistakes: Failing to weigh up the pros and cons of different ways of grouping activities, and failing to review these periodically.

7. (Looking at individual jobs) *Why does this job exist? What is its holder supposed to contribute to the organization? What are his responsibilities?*

Unless these questions are asked jobs may be created that are unnecessary, or, more commonly, may survive after the need has passed, as in the story about the man who asked why there was a man in the gunnery team who apparently had nothing to do and was told, 'Oh! He is there to hold the horses.'

It is particularly important to be clear about the purpose of a job, and the nature of its responsibilities, when deciding who would be suitable to appoint to it. Such clarity can also contribute to job satisfaction, as most people feel happier if they know what it is they are supposed to be doing. Investigation may show that the duties of a particular job are seen quite differently by the holder, his boss, his colleagues and his subordinates. This may be due, at least in part, to a failure to define the purpose of the job.

Common mistake: Fuzzy thinking about the responsibilities of individual jobs.

8. (Looking at individual jobs) *What is it like to be in this job? What are its strains, stresses and satisfactions?*

Managers rarely think enough about what it is like to work in a particular job. They need to do so in order to understand how people may react to it, and what the effect of these reactions will be on job performance. Research has taught us that quite different personalities may react in the same way to a particular job, and that reorganizing the job can change these reactions. The aim should be to design jobs that people will be interested in doing well.

Common mistake: Thinking too little about what it is like

*to work in particular jobs and of the need to take this
into account when designing jobs.*

9. *What effects does the form of organization have on
   people's relations with each other?*

Research has shown us that one method of organization
can create frictions and antagonisms between different individuals and groups, while another can encourage people to co-operate with each other. This is a lesson that is
worth remembering wherever technology permits of alternative methods of work organization.

*Common mistake: Failing to realize that the form of or-
ganization chosen can have repercussions on individual
and group behaviour, and that these should be taken into
account when considering the advantages and disadvantages of alternative methods of organizing work.*

10. *What are the relations like between line and staff
    departments?*

Complaints of friction between line and staff department are common, yet much can be done to encourage
good working relations between the two groups. Organizational clarity of the relationship is important. What is
the specialist supposed to do? Who does he report to?
Is he there only to advise, or are there some areas where
he is responsible for deciding what should be done? These
questions should be asked and clearly answered. Important, too, are the attitudes of the two groups to each
other. The staff should see their role as that of professional advisers to clients. Management should learn how
to draw on this professional knowledge without abdicating

responsibility. The relationship is one that often improves with time as the two groups get more used to working with each other.

Common mistake: Poor staff–line relations leading to inefficient use of specialist resources.

11. *What are managerial relations like?*

The effectiveness of an organization will depend, to a considerable extent, on the relations between individual managers. Do they work well together, or are they distracted by personal jealousies and power struggles? Some friction is likely, and is probably healthy, but power struggles can be harmful to the pursuit of common objectives. The head of the organization should try to ensure that arguments are not conducted in a win-or-lose atmosphere.

Common mistake: Managers who pursue their sectional interests rather than identify with a common purpose.

12. *Are people getting the information they need?*

There are all too many ways in which communications can be unsatisfactory. There may be too much information, too little, or it may be the wrong kind. Managers may be flooded with paper which they have no time to read, or even to distinguish what matters and what does not. Managers may feel that their time is wasted in meetings that are too frequent and too lengthy. Or there may be the opposite complaints, that one never knows what is going on; that decisions are taken that affect one, but one is not consulted, nor even told about them. It is still worse where one receives the wrong kind of information;

market analyses that are misleading, figures that are so out of date that they are not a good guide to action, or information that is deliberately selected so as to give too rosy a picture of what is happening.

Information often has to be passed from one person to another, or from one part of the organization to another. The official channels may be slow and inefficient. Status differences may be a barrier to the free exchange of information. Then there are all the problems that arise from the fact that what I say may not be what you hear, so that the information may get more and more distorted as it passes up or down the hierarchy.

Common mistake: Too little attention to what information is needed and to what is the most efficient way of communicating it.

13. *What thought is being given to career planning for management?*

What experience should managers have and what are the best ways for them to get it? These questions should be asked in all medium-sized and large organizations. The kind of experience that managers have will be partly determined by the form of organization. For example, young managers are likely to get more responsibility in decentralized organizations than in centralized ones.

The extent to which departments or establishments are self-contained, each with its own career structure, will affect the opportunities that young men and women will have to get a wider view of the organization. The danger of departmental or occupational career ladders is that managers will tend to have a narrow viewpoint, which can later be a handicap when they get to the top and have to view the organization as a whole.

Common mistake: Paying too little attention to career patterns and giving too little thought to the kind of experience that they provide.

Finally, there are contrasting faults of over- and under-organization, both of which may exist in different parts of the same company.

14. *Where is there too little systematization?*

Many organizations, particularly those that have grown rapidly, have too little formalization. Policies are not defined, people do not know what they should be doing, too little effort has been given to trying to devise standardized ways of dealing with certain activities. The result is muddle and uncertainty.

Common mistake: Too little attention to trying to systematize the work to be done.

15. *Where is there too much formalization and unnecessary red tape?*

This is an appropriate mistake with which to end because it is the popular idea of what is wrong with many large organizations. There is a tendency for those that are already highly formalized to develop systems, forms and procedures for their own sake rather than for the purpose they should be serving. New committees, new procedures may be needed, but all too often the old ones are not reviewed to see if they still serve a useful purpose. Managers may become infatuated with orderliness, thus forgetting the value of flexibility.

Common mistakes: An over-enthusiasm for trying to systematize the work to be done and the procedures to be followed, and a failure to review periodically the relevance of existing procedures.

Select Bibliography for the Manager

Plenty of books on organization contain long bibliographies. This is a highly selected list of books that the author's post-experience management students have found helpful.

GENERAL BOOKS

E. F. L. Brech, *Organization: The Framework of Management*, 2nd edn (London, Longmans, Green, 1965) pp. 561. Only for the serious-minded; useful appendix on the history of organizational thought.

Ernest Dale, *Organization* (New York, American Management Association, 1967) pp. 368. Primarily concerned with structure.

P. F. Drucker, *The Practice of Management* (London, Heinemann, 1955 (paperback, Pan, 1968, pp. 479). Only partly about organization, but included as it is one of the best and most readable.

J. A. Litterer, *Organization: Structure and Behavior* (New York, Wiley, 1963) pp. 418. Collection of articles and extracts, mainly by social scientists.

J. O'Shaughnessy, *Business Organizations* (London, Allen & Unwin, 1966) pp. 263. Useful description of different organizational theories.

John M. Pfiffner and Frank P. Sherwood, *Administrative Organization* (Englewood Cliffs, Prentice-Hall, 1960). Still one of the best general textbooks; is clearly written.

A number of well-known books on organization which should be read by graduate business students are not included, as they are too heavy-going for the busy manager.

BOOKS ON PARTICULAR ASPECTS (mainly research studies)

Many important books are excluded because they are hard to read.

Tom Burns and G. M. Stalker, *The Management of Innovation* (London, Tavistock, 1961). Important research study, but heavy-going in places. Popular version, Honor Croome, *Human Problems of Innovation,* Problems of Progress in Industry, no. 5 (Department of Scientific and Industrial Research, H.M.S.O., 1960 (pamphlet)).

Melville Dalton, *Men Who Manage: Fusions of Feeling and Theory in Administration* (Wiley, 1959) pp. 317. A frank study of management behaviour.

Robert H. Guest, *Organizational Change: The Effect of Successful Leadership* (London, Tavistock, 1962).

Herbert Kaufman, *The Forest Ranger: A Study in Administrative Behavior* (Baltimore, Johns Hopkins, 1960) pp. 259. An unusually good description of the working of one organization.

P. R. Lawrence and J. W. Lorsch, *Organization and Environment: Managing Differentiation and Environment* (Harvard University, 1967, pp. 279). Short account of research into differences in organization and their reasons.

Harold J. Leavitt, *Management Psychology* (University of Chicago, rev. edn, 1964) pp. 437. Most readable account of human relations in organizations.

Douglas McGregor, *The Human Side of Enterprise* (New York, McGraw-Hill, 1960) pp. 246. Famous *and* readable.

Leonard R. Sayles, *Managerial Behavior: Administration in Complex Organizations* (New York, McGraw-Hill, 1964) pp. 269. A good account of different types of managerial relations.

Joan Woodward, *Industrial Organization: Theory and Practice* (London, Oxford University Press, 1965) pp. 281. Research report on the relationships between the type of technology and the form of organization.

Index

Absenteeism, 31
accountability, 97, 116
Acton Society Trust, 102, 117
administratively responsible, 100
American Management Associa-
    tion, 51, 138, 147
appointment diaries, 167
Argyris, C., 30, 38
authority
    advantages and disadvantages of
        using, 87
    decline in, 88
    formal, 81–2, 87, 93, 120
    functional, 17, 103
    line, 34
    and responsibility, 5, 85, 111

Baker, A. W., 38
Bamforth, K. W., 46, 56
Bales, R., 71, 75
Baxtern, B., 185
behaviour
    studies of top management,
        131–2
Behavioural School, see Human
    Relations School
Blau, P. M., 65, 75, 123, 135
boundaries
    departmental, 119
    more fluid, 193, 197, 200–1
    system, 13
Brech, E. F. L., 21, 169, 215
British Civil Service, 145
British Tabulating Machines, 198
Brown, W., 154, 169
Burns, T., 119, 125, 130, 135, 216

canteen, xiii, 40, 44
career ladders, 170, 173, 183
career patterns, 170, 173–81, 183,
    212
    changes in, 194–5, 200–2
    effect on loyalties, 175–6
    entry point for potential man-
        agers, 174
    initial training, 175, 184
    job differences, 178

later entrants, 174
planning, 173, 177, 184, 195, 202,
    212
transfers between departments,
    176, 184
width of, 175–6
centralization, 60–1, 77, 137, 149
    advantages and disadvantages,
        142–4, 149
    and computers, 148
    changes in policy, 140, 144
    comparisons of, 138, 149
    trends, 147
change, rate of, 10, 65, 74, 98, 120,
    140, 149, 188, 199–200, 202,
    205
changes affecting organizations
    full employment, 189, 199, 201–3
    growth of state intervention, 187,
        198–9, 202–3
    growth of trade union interven-
        tion, 187, 198–9, 202
    more education, 189, 199, 201–3
    one world, 188–9, 199, 201–3
    rapid technical change, 188, 199,
        201–2
changes within organizations
    career patterns, 195, 201–2
    decline in hierarchical differ-
        ences, 196, 200–3
    increasing size, 190–1, 200–2
    increasing specialization, 195,
        200–3
    international corporation, 191,
        195–6, 199–203
    more fluid boundaries, 193,
        200–3
    staff composition, 193, 200–2
Chapple, E. D., 35, 39
China, 188
    managers in, 80
Christian names, use of, 126
Classical school, 4–7, 10, 16–19,
    37, 56, 85
coal industry, 141
coal-mining, longwall method, 46
code of conduct, 130

committees, 67–71, 166
    advantages, 67–70
    disadvantages, 70
    improving efficiency of, 68
    time spent in, 68
communications
    barriers to, 86, 125, 211–12
    failures in, 64
    lateral, 134
    managerial, 120
    restricting, 66
    span of control, effects on, 54
    written compared with spoken,
        165
computer
    control of, 50
    data bank, 14
    department, xii, 40, 100
    study of their use, 113
    system, 13–15
computers, impact on management,
    107, 178
conflict
    between departments, 61–2, 74
    between group and local inter-
        ests, 60–1
    between sales and production,
        61–2
control
    advantages of centralization, 143,
        149
    formalization, 156
    framework for, 88
    span of, 52–6, 81, 93
co-ordination, 4, 48, 58–73
    causes of problems in, 59–63, 74
    chain of command, 65–6, 74
    committees, 67–71, 74
    grouping, 66–7, 74
    informal discussion, 71, 75
    projects, 73
co-ordinator, 73–4
corporate planners, 27
cosmopolitan and local, 110
critical path analysis, 64
Croome, H., 216

Dale, E., 34, 39, 56, 70, 75, 104,
    147, 150, 215
Dalton, M., 169, 216
Davis, R. C., 38

deadlines, responsibility for meet-
    ing, 34
decision
    centre, 14
    -making, 127, 146–8
decisions
    and committees, 68–9
    at different levels, 141, 144–7
    knowledge for, 145–6
    need for review of, 208
    not always a conscious choice,
        147
    relative importance of, 145–6,
        207
    theory different from practice,
        148–9
delegation, 84, 137, 140, 207
    criteria for, 144–7
Department of Employment and
    Productivity, 44
Department of Health and Social
    Security, 201
departmental boundaries, 119
departmentalization, see grouping
Dickson, W. J., 21
divisionalization, 51–2, 55
Drucker, P., 33, 39, 215

educated population, 189, 199, 201
electricity industry, 141
electronic data processing, see
    computer
employment, full, 190, 195, 199,
    201–3
English Electric, 198

Fayol, G. H., 20
Fleishman, E. A., 185
formalization 26–7, 35–7, 151–69,
    213
    adaptation to change, 159, 169
    advantages of, 154–7
    appointments, 167–8
    avoiding dangers of, 159–61, 168
    balancing order and flexibility,
        151
    control, 156–7
    degree of, 151, 168
    description of, 158
    differences between organiza-
        tions, 155

formalization (*cont'd*)
differences within organizations, 151–2
disadvantages of, 157–60, 169
equity, 157
establishment of policies, 152–3
factors determining the amount of, 156–7
initiative, effects on, 158
insensitivity, 159
ossification, 160
provides security and certainty, 155
rules, 161–2, 169
speed and efficiency, 156
types of, 161–9
value in defining area of freedom, 154
when to formalize, 153, 159–60
Friedmann, G., 30–1, 38
functions, definition, 56

Glacier Metal, 154
Glickman, A. S., 185
Gouldner, A. W., 110, 117
graduates, competition for, 173
Granick, D., 169
group services, 60
grouping, 40–56, 208
criteria for, 48–51, 55
customers, 44–5, 49, 55
functions, 42–3, 47–8, 54
place, 45–7, 51, 55
process, 56
product or services, 41–2, 46–7, 54
purpose, 56
time, 45–6, 55
groups, studies of small, 65, 71
Guest, R. H., 216

Hacon, R. J., 184–5
Hahn, C., 185
Hawthorne studies, 6, 20
Heckman, I. L., 135
Herzberg, F., 39
Hickson, D. J., 150
Hinings, C. R., 150
hospital matrons, and inspection, 179
hospitals, xiv, 51, 62, 72, 97, 125, 167

changes in general, 200–1
district general, 201
House of Commons, 145
Human Relations School, 6, 9, 16, 20–1, 91
Huneryager, S. G., 135
Hutter, L., 135

I.B.M., 31, 198
I.C.I., 32
Industrial Expansion Act, 198
information
flow, 14, 18
formal, 15
informal, 15
needs, 15
inspection, 28
international companies, 191, 194–6, 198–203
International Computers Ltd, 198–200
International Computers and Tabulators, 198

job
descriptions, 5, 33–7, 50, 165, 182
enlargement, 30–2
enrichment, 30–2, 207
guides to design of, 32–3, 209–10
responsibilities, 208–9
rotation, 114
specification, 165, 181
stress, 7–8, 13, 17, 209
jobs
knowledge of, 27
specialization, 25–9, 37–8, 194, 200–2
tradition, 26
training value, 175, 179

Kahn, R. L., 83, 94–5
Katz, D. K., 95, 131, 136
Kaufman, H., xv, 66, 104, 150, 160, 169, 216
Koontz, H., 117

Lawrence, P. R., 21, 136, 216
leadership
style, 87, 91–4
type of, 80

Leavitt, H. J., 21, 87, 150, 180, 185, 216
Levy, S., 135
Lewis, R., 135
Likert, R., 91, 95
line and staff, 115–17, 210. *See also* managers and specialists
    definitions, 96
line boss, 100
Litterer, J. A., 215
Lorsch, J. W., 21, 216
loyalty, corporate, 130–1, 135, 177

McClelland, W. G., 173, 177–8, 181, 184–5
McGregor, D., 30, 38, 111, 116–17, 216
McKinsey, 113, 117
management
    autocratic, 91, 189
    -by-objectives, 88
    changes in composition of, 172
    computers, impact on, 107, 180
    different skills at different levels, 177–80
    hierarchy, 172
    philosophy, 36, 38, 132, 141, 149
    standard of efficiency, 194
management succession, 170–84
    age of promotion to top management, 180
    balancing needs of jobs and individuals, 181–3
    career patterns, 173–81, 183–4
    determining future needs, 171–3
    later entrants, 174
    organizational problems of, 170–84
    philosophy of management development, 182
    promotion opportunities, 173–4
    training value of different jobs, 179, 184
manager, as a decision-taker, 14, 15
managerial relations, 118–35, 211
    changes in, 119–20
    differences between jobs, 123–5, 133–4
    power structure, 127–30
    types of, 120–3

managers
    dependence on others, 118, 134
    dining-rooms, 72, 82
    impact of government intervention, 186–8
    personality differences, 123–4
    use of time, 182
    working patterns, 24
managers and specialists, 91–117, 210. *See also* line and staff
    dangers of management abdication, 99, 108
    differences in acceptability, 106–8, 116
        jobs, 110
        outlook, 109–10, 116
        staff functions, 106
    improving relations, 111–17
    mutual criticisms, 108–9
    organization, 97–106, 115–16
    outside specialists, use of, 105
    problems of relationship, 99–106
materials controller, 28
Mayo, E., 6
merger, 133, 206
Michigan, University of, Institute of Social Research, 91
Ministry of Technology, 198
Mooney, J. D., 20
morale, 6, 9
motivation, 87, 91

National Coal Board, 103
National Health Service, 188, 200
National Industrial Conference Board, 117
nationalization, 141
nationalized industries, 157

objectives, xi, xv, 9, 17, 34, 58, 86, 94, 133, 141, 155, 204–6
    management-by-, 88
O'Donnell, C., 117
oil companies, 191
operational research, 13–15, 27
order and flexibility, *see* formalization
organic system of management, 125
organization
    balance between advantages and disadvantages, xii, 77, 143–4, 181–4

organization (*cont'd*)
  bureaucratic, 36, 181–5
  changing, 78, 172, 186–203
  chart, 46–7, 163–6
  common mistakes, 205–13
  complexity of, 3
  deficiencies, xi
  effects on behaviour, 8, 12, 210
  effects of growth, xi, 28, 37
  formal, 4–5, 8–9, 19–20
  goals, 130. *See also* objectives
  hierarchical, 65–6, 196, 200, 202
  illustrations of, xii
  increasing size, 190–1, 194, 197,
    199–202
  informal, 8
  loyalty, 130–1, 135, 176–**7**
  manuals, 165
  meaning of, xiv–xv
  and methods, 25
  principles, of, 4
  size differences in, xi, 36, 133,
    140, 151, 169, 181–4, 202
  study of, xi
  varies with the situation, 205
O'Shaughnessy, J., 215
Oxford Centre for Management
    Studies, xi

patient care, changes in, 188
Paul, W. J., 39
Petersen, E., 56
Pfiffner, J. M., 215
Philips, N.V., 32, 39
Plowman, E. G., 56
population, changes in, 206
Post Office, 157
power
  battles, 128
  structure, 127–30, 134
Power-Samas, 198
press release, 64
production management, 178–80
productivity, 9–10, 12
professional
  association, 187–8, 201
  skill, problems of rewarding, 181
  standards, 100
professionalism, 27, 37
professionalization, growth of, 194
project teams, 73–4, 114, 117

Pugh, D. S., 138, 150

rank, 81–2, 93, 166
Regional Hospital Boards, 201
Reiley, A. C., 20
relationships
  functional, 97–9
  trading, 121–3, 134
  work-flow, 121, 134
  See also under subject heading
responsibilities, definition of, 5, 17,
    19–20
retirement policies, 160
Rice, A. K., 56
Robertson, K. B., 39
Roethlisberger, F. L., 21
Rosen, E., 135
rules, 161–2, 169

sack, right to, 81–2
Sadler, P. J., 93–5
sales executives, characteristics of,
    124–5
Sayles, L., 35, 39, 120–3, 134–5,
    216
Scott, W. R., 65, 75, 123, 135
selection procedures, 173
Shell, 195
Sherwood, F. P., 215
shift-working, 45–6
Simon, H., 21
site agent, 17–18
social distance, 82
specialization, 25–9, 37, 43
  growth of, 194, 200–3
staff boss, 99, 115–16
Stalker, G. M., 119, 126, 130, 135,
    216
state intervention, 186, 198–200,
    202
status, 72, 81–2, 93, 113, 126
  symbols, 166
Stewart, R., 57, 75, 135, 185
superior–subordinate relationships,
    79–95
  cultural background to, 80–1
  leadership style, 91–2
  organizational influences on,
    81–3, 93
  problems in, 70–91, 94
  time spent in, 94

systems
  analysis, 148
  approach to organization, 10–20
  defined, 10
  information, 11, 13–15
  social, 11–12, 21
  socio-technical, 50

tasks, definition and analysis of, 4
Tavistock Institute of Human Relations, 12, 50
technical change, rate of, 188, 199–200, 203
technology, type of, affecting organization, 10
Theory X and Theory Y, 30–1
Tillman, R., Jr, 75
time-and-motion study, 28
trade union
  change in activities, 187
  intervention, 187, 198–201, 202
trading relationship, 121–2, 134
Trickett, J. M., 56
Trist, E. L., 46, 56
Truman, D. B., 139, 150

Turner, C., 150
typing pool, xiii, 62

Unilever, 195
U.S. Forest Service, xiv, 66, 104–5, 160
United States Presidency, 35
Urwick, L., 20, 52, 57

waitresses, 7
Western Electric Co., 6
Whisler, T., 150, 180, 185
Whyte, W. F., 21, 136
Wilson, A. T. M., 178, 185
Woodward, Joan, 28, 38, 64–5, 75, 216
work, see jobs
work-flow relationship, 121, 134
work structuring, 32
workers, rise in expectations, 189
works management, 178–9
world
  one, 188–9, 199, 201–3
  wide career planning, 195
  wide training, 195